The Spirits I See: The Discovery of a Medium

By

Cindy Kueczynski

Seeing Spirits: The Discovery of a Medium

By

Cindy Kueczynski

Table of Contents

Forward

I rolled over in the middle of the night and sensed I was not alone. It's a feeling that somehow someone or something has made their way into my house, passed our two dogs, unnoticed by my over active cats and has now found their way to me. If I open my eyes my fears will become reality, as they have so many times before. To have that child like feeling that if I opened my eyes someone may be in the room, a total stranger in my space. Like a small child I fight the urge to pull the covers over my head, yet my eyes being curious opened against my better judgment. The outline of a person appeared at the bottom of my bed. I kicked my legs and slid my body back into my husbands. I made no sound, after all this was not the fist time I have been through this. The outline clarified as I now could make out the silhouette to be of an elderly woman. I could sense her confidence and wisdom. Her white hair rested down her back as I could see it move as she lifted up her arm. She seemed to be wearing a black dress that had a certain comfort and 17th century style to it. She spoke and as she did it seemed to make an echo sound "Burn a black Candle", "Burn a black candle" She repeated her words as she clearly became more agitated as she moved closer. I looked into her eyes which were shadowed because of the darkness as I struggled to bring the woman more into focus as I squeezed my pillow tighter. I was thinking that maybe by focusing on her that somehow that would make the image disappear... She now became clearer and a more determined tone was present in her voice. She now was standing by the side of my bed. Her hand was still reached out; I could now see that she seemed to have a pair of tapered candles lying across her hand. With her being so close, I became a bit unsure if she was real or a vision. With the tone in her voice becoming stronger, I was not sure if she was closing in to harm me or if she was simply just trying to let me know the urgency in what she was saying. My screams awoke my husband which at this time in our marriage he was use to. The woman was gone and my husband did not see anyone. I think my scream must have sent her back into her spirit realm. Or did it?

Some nights I made my way to the computer in the middle of the night. This was way out of a normal routine. I tried to reason with myself, to just go lay back down. But I ended up starting a pot of coffee and soon found myself lost in the middle of writing. The images of all my spirit visitors came to replay in my mind during the duration of writing this book. I thought it would be useful that people know that it's okay to be a little different. In the society that we currently live in, there is always someone claiming prejudice against them. Yet not everyone is allowed to, because the world is only set up to allow race issues to be the bonds for prejudice. People are individuals and they can look at a person and not like them for more reasons then their color. Most people keep their gifts and visions to themselves. I had a lot of spirit visitor's during the writing of the book, some were old and some were new.... There is nothing easy about writing a book, but when it's your first one you really don't think of that. Writing the book is the easy part, having someone take you serious because of the nature of the subject is not so simple. Finding a publisher with nothing but your best interest at heart, well that is another thing. . I would not learn till years later how false promises and so called contracts took my words and profited from them, yet left the words within the covers. This book is spirit guided and written. Why I decided to write a book or why I thought that after all these years, now is the time... Maybe just maybe I could explain what I go through and witness that this could help someone else.

I couldn't figure out why I would even want to write a book now? At the time I decided to start this book, I was working full time, and managing a lot of other projects with the dream of opening my own store. In an instantaneous flash of insight, I "saw" myself helping others by recording all of my paranormal experiences in a book that would tell my story. I realized there were probably other people out there having similar "spirit" experiences and who were undoubtedly looking for answers to questions like "What was that ?" "Are they evil?" "Should I be afraid?" "Am I nuts" and "Why me?" When I thought about it after it was done I think the desire to help others if only in a little way would perhaps encourage them to grow their own gift.

Spirit written books are not uncommon; this has been done before. I don't know how the other

4

authors wrote while under spirit guidance, but for me, sometimes my visions appear to me and give me something to write, like the woman telling me to buy a black candle. It just seems that the words just start flowing. I don't plan how and why I just allow my fingers to type. The energy and time that suddenly appeared for me to achieve this was a blessing.

I hope that with this book others can be helped to be more aware and receptive to the messages that we get from our spirit guides. Everyone has spirit guides, whether they call them by that name or not, whether they choose to believe in them or not. They are always with us; their purpose is to help and support us. Their presence provides us with a feeling of security; that we are not alone and that the end of this life may not be quite as final as we have been led to believe. If you have the gift you better use it or you will lose it. If you do not acknowledge it you are wasting a beautiful gift, one that makes you special and unique. You are one of the few voices for the other side.

Over the time span of writing this book, I received many emails from people some of whom are very afraid of "picking up" an evil or negative spirit. Because of misguided advice passed down by someone who may believe it to be evil. I just could not believe how such a wonderful experience could be treated like a disease. I have also heard the "horror stores" about pernicious spirits and even watched many movies that portray them as just that. The sorts of spirits which appear to me just seem to be asking me for help; warning me of an upcoming death, pushing me to achieve something, showing me something that may take me to say "Happy Birthday" to someone, or just showing me a stream of events that I believe lead up to their death.

The events put forth in this book are some of the events that I have experienced throughout my life so far; I have come to consider them as a gift. Admittedly at times, these "visions" have emotionally felt like being thrown against a wall! But it is my sincere hope that this book helps others unleash their own potential and to enable them to also view similar incidents as a gift and ultimately, a privilege. I would never trade the experiences for anything and have even gone so far as to encourage my daughters to definitely work with someone to develop and enhance her own gift, if she ever has the opportunity.

Chapter one

The Beginning

When ever you hear about people who are able to communicate with spirits you may also hear their story about a Near Death Experience "NDE". When a tragic accident attempts to claim the life of someone as they start to fade out of this life, some say that they seen someone who may be related or a friend. While my father was sitting in his hospital room being treated for cancer, he pointed to the door to the bathroom and said "look who it is." However what happens if it's just not your time. What happens if the accident is truly just that? You travel through the tunnel following your guide as the light becomes brighter; as you get closer the light touches you. Does this light now bless you with the ability to communicate with spirits when you return to your natural state? I believe this may be how one gets an advance Psychic ability or it awakens to the clairvoyant abilities. . I believe that everyone is born with a certain amount of Psychic abilities. Trusting your gut feeling is an example of a psychic ability. You have heard about situations where the phone rings and you just know who is calling before you answer it? If you were to work with that part of your senses then you can grow this sense and stay open, but it can only get to a certain point for most people. I truly believe that a Medium is one who spirits reach out to and show things. The medium is the one that becomes the liaison between both realms. Someone who is Psychic is not able to train to become a Medium, but all Mediums are natural Psychic's. The Medium usually has inherited the gift. If you know someone who has this gift I am sure that you will find that they have some other family member that has had these experiences. That is if they choose to talk about it. There is still a generation that believes it to be a forbidden subject.

There are a few capabilities that define Mediumship. One does not have to be gifted with all three to be a medium... Actually most mediums do not experience messages through all three channels.. To hear, see and feel spirit, this is what a medium does. Clairaudience is the ability to hear spirits. I have actually had a spirit appear to me in day light and say "Are you ready?" Others may hear a whispering. Clairvoyance is the ability to see spirits, and Clairsentience sensing spirits presences and their thoughts... This can be viewing an event within your minds eye that the spirit wishes to show you for one reason or another.

. . This can be shut down by simply learning to ignore it over time. Or you can enhance it. When you get your gift this way, it is different then those with normal psychic abilities.

NDE, some scientists say, is just an electrical "downloading" of the brain's data as the body dies; others say it is a hallucination... If we look at our brain waves as electrical and we reach a different frequency, we become more open to other things that may be operating at that same level. Could this be why some of us see spirits? Though experiencing a NDE is not a necessity to acquire this gift, in my case the NDE, when I found out about it helped me begin to understand "The Beginning." This is a point to begin looking at why I am seeing what I see.

My own NDE experience happened when I was near the age of two. At that age, of course, I had not paid much attention to anyone who talked about death, after all I had enough visitors at night and I did not need to have anything else to keep me up at night. I didn't learn about spirit communication until I was an adult. Then I actually started connecting the dots and pursing understanding my gift more in detail. Trying to find out what the terms I was coming across meant. I first came to understand the meaning of a Near Death Experience" after I had a reading by a Psychic prior to me writing this book. Like many others who want to know what the future holds and to experience the fun and fulfill the curiosity. I had contacted her to set up a reading. During the reading she did tell me a lot of basic information that could easily fit into anyone's life if t hey twisted and looked really hard. For Instance I was told that my Grandma was looking over me and to validate this she said that I had a habit of turning the rings on my fingers. As I said "No" I don't really do that, she quickly corrected me for the audience and said "believe me yes you do" A lot of what she told me I could not relate to. She did not continue to relay personal information about my childhood, which I did not understand nor could I validate for her... After the reading I read through my notes and still could not relate a lot of it. I called my mother and got this very interesting story, of which after all these years, I was unaware, had even occurred. By the story she told I guess it is not something you really want to pass down to your kids as they get older.

My Mom told me that one day, when I was a baby she had gone to the store and left my father watching my two older brothers and me. A "game" of some kind was on TV when she left. Dad, being a hard core sports fan, never missed a televised game for anything. He would lounge in front of the television flipping back and forth to any other channel showing another game. He would stay there lying on the floor on his side for as long as a game was on. His standing rule was to never be disturbed; any disruptions during a game angered him easily Being German my father yelled a lot. When I say a lot, I mean a lot then he yelled a lot and he yelled extremely loud. There was no talking to him at this point. We would just simply clear the room as quickly as possible. This was the way he was all the way up to his death.

Mom guessed that after she had left, I must have been crying, because at some point, a pillow was placed near my head she assumed, to muffle my cries so he could continue to hear the game on TV. (I know this sounds pretty bad, but not all people are good with kids; I think in his younger years, Dad was one of those people.) When my mother came back from the store, she found me with the pillow on top of my head! Shocked, she yanked the pillow off my face, and noticed I was barely breathing. She told me that I gasped deeply for air. She also remembered how frightfully red my face was and I was sweat soaked and sobbing. She shuddered to think what might have happened, if she had been not returned back when she did what would have happened. I think that during some point there had to be a commercial and dad would have check on me right? That traumatic experience, I truly believe, was also responsible for triggering my asthma; a chronic condition which has bothered me since before kindergarten.

The earliest visions that I remember were when I was five years old. I can clearly recall them still today. I see them still the same that I seen them then. These first spirits were truly unique because every night the same spirits would come. Now when I get spirits that drop in, most of the time they are different spirits and some I don't know. During those years my Dad was in the Navy and he was stationed overseas in Japan for three years. I had two older brothers Freddie and Ronnie and my youngest brother Rusty had just been born prior to my father heading off for Japan. We all moved in with my grandma on American street in Bridgeton, NJ, I still believe that this location has active spirit activity in the upper far bedroom and the attic. The basement, I would not venture to so what stirs there I don't know, and with two older brothers who scared me when ever they could I would be afraid to go down there in fear of them locking me down there. Because of my visions I was the blunt of a lot of their jokes when they got bored at night. Neither of these brothers ended up with the gift. At least that's what they say.

My first vision was at Grandmas house during the time we stayed with her. It was a solid two-story house that she split into two apartments. There was an attic and basement. Grandma owned the split duplex and rented the other side out. I was lucky though because I had a room to myself. It was the last room at the end of a long wooden hallway. This was my Grandma's room but she stopped using it after my grandfather died. Or perhaps my asthmatic coughing kept the whole house awake, so they had to isolate me; but I happily had my own bedroom as a result.

Growing up with asthma back then was horrible. No medication was given to me for about the first year I had asthma. As a result, I often did not sleep at night I would sit up at night rocking and loudly gasping for breath. The pounding in my chest hurt as I struggled to catch each breath. When I coughed the air was harder to come by and my chest was so soar as I fought for every breath. When the house went quiet and everyone else drifted off to sleep. Humming would start to fill the room. The humming would get louder and louder. The humming would go on for a while before the darkness would fall over the room. I slept with a night light on, however the light seemed to fade out as the room began to change colors. The room went from dark to a light red. I remember thinking how loud, quiet really was.

I blinked my eyes, trying to correct my sight of the strange red haze in my room and all around me. In the far corner of the room near the window there was an old wooden dresser that once belonged to my grandfather, who I never got to meet. He burned in his car after an accident caused by a drunk political figure. A tall figure appeared as I started to focus on it, I could see a woman. The first times she came to see me her back was to me. I stopped rocking myself back and forth and seemed to freeze in place, the hair on the back of my neck stood up and tingled. I tried to call out for Mom in a low voice, but it was hard to speak. I could open my mouth, but nothing would come out.

Her dress had a jumper or an apron over it tied in the back around her waist and her neck. The dress was long and flowing everything was white, the window was opened behind where she stood and the curtains blew behind her .She did not speak she would stand there in front of the dresser and fold clothing or linen. The room stayed red the whole time she went about her work. I watched her till my eyes grew heavy. The quietness continued as she folded the clothes.

My breathing seemed to calm as I settled down and did not concentrate on struggling to catch a breath. I never realized this till many years later that when I sat up in my bed and rocked myself back and fourth, quietly watching her, my breathing became more manageable I would finally lay my head back on the headboard and fell asleep. I was still sitting up during my sleep but her being there set a calmness over me that still today when someone is folding clothes I feel this unbelievable calmness come over me. I understand now that she at first only showed me the front of her because this was all new to me and I really was in no condition to understand what was going on. I had to be able to handle the things I was witnessing. I believe that I only experience what I am able to understand. Seriously, imagine this happening to you. What would you do? I was only five. I know how I would react because they still today can catch me off guard. How do you seriously think you would act your first time? She was there to help me create a breathing rhythm for my asthma. At this time of my life I was just too young for anything more.

Night after night I watched wide-eyed, as she stood at the dresser folding clothes and putting them away into the dresser. I could hear the sound of the drawers opening and closing. I watched as she snapped out each piece of clothing before she folded it. She was now standing sideways too. I could see her in more details. She did not speak and she did not seem to look at me or even notice me.

The start of the humming before the room turned red would be the one part that scared me the most. I would hide under the blanket or pillow afraid to look up. I hoped the humming would go away and that I would not see the spirit that night. I know that I never really looked forward to it even if I knew she was not there to hurt me. It was just having this stranger in my room that just scared me. That split second the spirit appears made my head tingle and my nose felt funny.. At bed time every night I would try so hard to get my mom to leave the big hallway light on instead of my little night light. She would not allow me to have it on. If my brothers heard me ask, well that would start them trying to scare me at night.

As the routine began I didn't talk about the lady visiting me on the nights she came. It was just another event that I grew up with. I believe I tried telling my mom once and my brothers heard me and they picked on me about it for many years after., well into my teens they still remembered it and would torment me. At night, shortly after the house settled down and the only glow in my room was a small night-light, I would sit in my bed rocking myself back and forth. The color in the room would start to change, adjusting the surrounding nighttime darkness into the now familiar color of red.

I learned quickly the sounds and sights would be followed by a peaceful feeling and the presents of the glowing lady. I never heard her speak. She just stayed within the same general area doing the same thing every night. After repeatedly seeing her, I was now quite accustomed to her and had gotten a feeling from her that I could relax more. I would sit and watch her for what seemed like hours. The whole time we lived in that house with Grandma, she never stopped visiting. I guess some kids have make believe friends that they have tea parties, have a play tend sleep over or maybe even color in their

11

favorite coloring book. Then there are people like me that see, hear, and feel spirits.

I never out grew my asthma, I adapted. I learned if I leaned against the wall or headboard, I could breathe a little easier and could finally drift off to sleep. I did not lie down to sleep, like normal children. Lying down to sleep caused so much breathing distress that it was just out of the question for me for many years in my youth. Day after day, I lived that way.

I credit the glowing lady with keeping me alive those nights at home when I struggled so to breathe. (Even now when I get sick, I find a certain sense of security and relaxation when someone is folding the laundry, as I lay in back with my pillows on the headboard. I never related that till I sat down to write this book; like I said this book is spirit guided. When my Dad completed his tour of duty in Japan, we finally did move from Grandma's. I never saw that glowing lady spirit again, that I can recall.

During the writing of this book while talking to my Mom, I mention the glowing lady from my childhood visions. She said she did not remember me talking about her and that this was the first time she knew about this particular vision. She said she wished that I would have told her and my grand mom. She sounded excited about it and I felt she was holding back. I was looking for confirmation and help with identifying her for this book. I had to say something at one time or another, after all my brothers did manage to know about it.

Whether I told anyone about the glowing lady as a child or not, I can now clearly remember. I saw her so often that she was nothing less then real to me. Her presence felt so normal and comforting that I may not have felt concerned enough to alert anyone; or maybe I thought everyone already knew about her. After all, if I could see her, then they must have seen her too.

My brothers still made fun of me. The "boogie man" was going to get me. Sometimes they even hid under my bed and grabbed at my feet. Once they reached a clothes hanger over the staircase as I came up it whispering "Hanger-hand man!" an act that I am sure kept me up all night scared.

12

I have a friend who is a psychic and a few years ago, I asked her to help me learn about the glowing lady. She communicated with this spirit for me, and revealed that the lady had been a nurse in her earthly life. She had liked helping children and had worked at a foster home where children lived until they were adopted. Her place of interment was in a graveyard that I passed daily going to and coming home from school.

There were often days, when walking to school, that my asthma bothered me so badly I thought I would not make it. With each step and gasping breath, the school seemed impossibly far away. I often could hardly move, but as I would pass the graveyard, my chest would stop aching and the familiar feeling of calmness felt in my bedroom, would overtake me. I some times sat down on the curve there to catch my breath before I continued on. Perhaps I "picked her up" on one of those walks to and from school.

The glowing lady was not the only presence in my grandmother's house. In the corner of Grandma's living room was a special chair. It was my grandfather's chair. Grandfather had passed away in a car accident when I was just an infant. A collision with a drunk driver had caused his car to overturn, trapping Grandfather inside, burning him alive. None of us kids would sit in this chair, we were all afraid that our grandfather was sitting in it.; I never saw him there, but still today, I remember thinking he was in that chair and I certainly did not want to sit on him.

Before we moved from Grandma's house, one of the last spirits I saw in that bedroom was a German shepherd. Out of the darkness, this dog jumped into my bedroom thru the window and onto my bed. He ran across my bed, shaking it as he ran across the foot of my bed. He did not see me, but I heard him panting as he excitedly hurrying as if someone had called him.

He then jumped off my bed and ran down the hallway. As he turned the corner, I could hear his claws scratching across the slippery wooden floor, and he disappeared out of sight. It all happened so fast that I didn't have time to do anything. As I describe this to you, in my mind I can still clearly see him, feel him, hear him and smell him.

The next morning, I told my Mom what I had seen during the night. She must have thought I had lost my mind with that one. I told her what I truly felt, and there was nothing else in the house that could have produced that same experience; we did not even own a dog, nor did our neighbors. The biggest thing about this vision is that my bedroom was on the 2nd floor. The memory of the dog that night is with my as clearly as that night.

The years seemed to go by quick when you get to looking back in time. My father passed of cancer. In the days before my Father's funeral, Mom had the bittersweet chore of going through some of his belongings. He didn't have much, but we all sat in the kitchen, tearfully going thru some of the family pictures. We wanted to place a few selected ones in my father's casket for the viewing. After making her choices, Mom gave me some to keep for myself; a few old black and whites, which we both thought would be suitable to pass down to my family. In that stack was a picture of a dog, a German shepherd, sleeping in a person's bed and covered up with a blanket, with his head resting on the pillow.

My eyes widened as I recognized the same bed-jumping German shepherd I had seen as a child. Don't ask me how I knew for sure, I just did and for the first time in my life my mom told me her story that this dog was her beloved family pet from her childhood. She had spoken about him at times when I was older and we moved to New Jersey but I had not made the connection until right then. Without a doubt in my mind, that *was* the same dog. Why I saw him when I was a child, I still do not know. I often think of my Grandmother and that house. After Grandmother died, the house was put up for sale by her kids. It still sits on American Avenue in Bridgeton, NJ. I wondered why my mom didn't mention she had a German Shepard when I told her about that dog running across my bed and down the hall.

My visions did not stop when we moved from that house. They continue to this day. I am not a psychic, and after 35 years of seeing people who have passed on, I still don't always know why they appear to me or what they want. But, I'm not the only one. Others in my family have the "gift" too.

My mother was born with a veil over her face. Back in those days, they thought that a veil over a child's face during birth was a special token for protection. Traditionally, birth veils were often saved and used by sailors as a protective charm when out to sea. But it was also thought to be an omen that the veiled child would display some psychic abilities later in life.

My mother did have the gift of what we thought was a psychic abilities as a little girl. She was able to "know" when someone was going to have an untimely death. She could just tell by the way the person would act. She described it as being unusually happy to her. She recalled that once when she was very young, she was with her mother and her aunt at a family gathering. Her aunt was laughing and acting overly silly, quite out of character and unlike her, it seemed to my mother. Just as Mom was watching and wondering what was wrong with her aunt, a quick vision of a field of flowers flashed before her eyes accompanied with the overpowering aroma of blooming flowers.

The scent was so convincing, she truly expected everyone else present could also smell them. She remembered tapping her mother on the hand. Her mother bent down to listen and she softly told her mother that her aunt was going to die soon. Her mother asked her what made her think that. She explained to her mother how she had seen the field of heavily scented flowers in her mind. My Mother was not familiar with flowers but she describes them in simple terms "purple flowers" with a real strong scent. She remembered that after a moment of mild surprise, her mother calmly whispered to back to her that she too had seen and smelled the very same thing. Her aunt did pass shortly after that.

My mother and her mother never spoke of the experience again. It was not something you would bring up back in the 1920's.

I only learned of Mom's experience with the "purple flowers" only after I too had the same experience and I called her often to tell her of my experiences and she would call me with hers.

One summer day while I was busy doing freelance work out of my home, an overpowering smell of flowers broke my concentration with a jolt. I looked up from my work and then looked all around me, not knowing what I would find. The scent was so strong that I decided to let in some fresh air by opening the bedroom windows.

I went to my bedroom to open the door to the room. Just as I turned the doorknob and pushed the door open, I was hit by a wave of dizziness and at the same time had a flash vision of a field of purple flowers! I blinked my watering eyes and the field of scented flowers, were gone.

This seemed to be to have been some sort of premonition, because a strong thought of my father popped into my head as the smell of the purple flowers faded from the room.

Anxious and with an unexplainable sense or urgency, I immediately picked up the phone to call home; compelled to warn Mom to make plans now for the days after Dad would pass away.

At that time, Father, who had been under treatment for cancer, had been in remission. As I made the phone call to Mother, I prayed this "purple flower" premonition would be proven wrong. He seemed to have beaten the cancer and had been looking and feeling better. Sadly, the remission turned out to be a short-lived victory. He passed away about six months later. The flash vision of the field of purple flowers had been correct.

For Mother and me, the field of scented purple flowers foretells an impending death. To me this was also proof that the gift was inherited from my mother. She had never told me of her visions until I began telling her about mine.

Another interesting incident Mom told me about happened to her shortly after her father had died.

As children when they were growing up in my grandmother's house, my mother and her sister shared a bed. This particular night, a few short weeks since their father's funeral, while she and her sister were in bed, they heard the familiar and immediately recognizable sound of their father's loud footsteps coming down the hallway towards them.

Mom said she squeezed her eyes shut tight and was terrified to open them. The footsteps grew louder as they neared and then stopped. Suddenly they both felt the bed move as he sat down onto the bed next to them!

This incident happened when they were in their early teens and although both Mother and my aunt are now nearing seventy years old, they both still carry on about it today. They still wonder whether he was just saying good-bye, or whether he was just letting them know that he was still with them by looking in on them at bedtime one last time. I wonder if perhaps at this point, he did not even know he was gone because his death was such a sudden and horrific accident.

Another incident, although weird, which stuck in Mom's memory, also happened around the time of her father's passing.

A few days after her father's funeral Mom went into the bathroom for some small item, and lo and behold, there on the toilet sat a human size skeleton! He sat holding onto the edge of the toilet seat with both bony hands and taking a momentary break from his business, he turned to look over at Mom.

She had been frightened at that time when she saw him, but now she laughs about this vision. I guess sometimes spirits can possess a sense of humor. Maybe it had just been his way of cheering her up, because after she had time to think about it, it seemed quite comical! I think I would have kept all the lights in the house turned on, after that experience!

My family, on my mother's side, has also had some pretty interesting things happen over the years. This next incident, however, was not comical in the least.

Family history about my great grandfather stated that he had been a miner of some sort. The story goes that he and his adult son were mining one day, when his son accidentally fell into a deep, abandoned mineshaft. Great Grandfather and the other miners tried valiantly to rescue the injured man, but they were unsuccessful.

As his son lay screaming from the excruciating pain, the miners tearfully struggled to keep my great grandfather restrained inside his truck in an effort to prevent him from hurting himself should he try to aid his fatally injured son. The young man's cries were so heart wrenching that a metal bucket was eventually lowered down over his head in a futile effort to muffle the desperate shrieks until mercifully, he finally expired from lack of oxygen.

Now that is just a downright horrible way to go! I can't imagine Great Grandfather's suffering that day at not being able to help his son, nor I imagine what his son suffered as he died.

Mom reluctantly told us of this disturbing piece of family history in response to a question I had the day we were sorting pictures for Father's funeral display.

While sorting through the photos with Mom that day, I had come across a picture of a young man and asked Mom who he was. When I told her I had seen him before, she seemed very surprised.

A few years before my father died, I had seen the man from the photo in a vision. He had appeared as a young man with a "glowing head" and stood beside my bed. I instantly knew he was related, but thought the "glowing head" may have been caused by his blonde hair; hair so blonde that it glowed. Blonde hair was common in our family and came from the German ancestry from Father's side.

But after hearing Mother's account of this man's tragic death, I now think the vision had a "glowing head" because that's where the miners placed the bucket; over his head in an attempt to muffle his screams. The vision of this man left an emotional impression of this event on me and it is as vividly connected to me as if I had actually been there. I can feel my great grandfather's wretched pain and inconsolable loss. It was said that he never really recovered from this. I can tell you that he was probably no the only one.

Mom's brother and sister have both had their share of visions also.

Mom remembers her sister telling her of an interesting event, which occurred after her sister's husband passed away and was, laid to rest.

A few days after her husband's funeral, my aunt went into her bedroom and was shocked to find him lying on their bed! Not being the screaming type, she gently put her hand on his chest, and gasped as she watched her hand pass right through him.

In retrospect, I think this was his way of letting her know "this was for real," that he was really gone. My aunt still talks about this vision. I now know that when you actually see a spirit or spirit guide, the impression will stay with you forever, as do my own.

Mom's brother once had a "late night wake up" by a Civil War soldier.

Dressed in the unmistakable Union blue and battle ready, the vision sat down on my uncle's bed and said, "Come on let's go," while trying to coax him out of the bedroom.

Because of the urgent tone in his voice, my uncle concluded that the soldier was on his way to battle, or was perhaps about to flee from a battle. The man stood hurriedly and with a backwards glance at my uncle, he left the bedroom. My uncle said he could feel the bed move as the stranger sat down on it and again as he got up to leave. This parallels the same thing I felt when the dog ran across the bed.

So it is possible to see them, hear them *and* feel them.

This soldier must have died abruptly (now called sudden death syndrome) and was not able to complete what he had intended; he did not realize he was gone, therefore his spirit lingers, as do the spirits of many of the men who died in the Civil War. They were so young. Do they all not realize they have passed on?

From among all my brothers and my only sister, there are only two of us, including me, who have the gift now.

Similarly, my brother Chuck had his gift appear after a NDE. My brother's gift is also like mine, but more intense. He is able to see spirits, but in addition, he can hear them and feel them touch him. Most notably, he can also interact with them by obtaining responses from them to his actions or questions. (When I started writing this book, I could not feel them but that has since changed.)

Chuck was about seven years old when he had his near death experience.

He and Dad were sitting at home in the living room eating a BLT (bacon, lettuce & tomato) sandwich while watching a game on TV. As he wolfed down a bite of sandwich, Chuck suddenly began to choke. Dad tried to help him, but to no avail and in a panic, shouted for Mom (did I mention the game was on?).

By the time Mom came into the room, Chuck was unable to talk or breathe and had begun to turn purple. Mom did the abdominal thrust maneuver, which sent the bacon flying out into the room. He still clearly remembers the incident like it was yesterday. He remembers the bacon as being the "fatty stuff" that Dad liked. For many years afterward, Chuck refused to eat bacon or similar fatty foods because he was so afraid of choking like that again.

It was shortly after that traumatizing event, that Chuck began to realize he had the "gift."

This gift received by my brother and me, comes with a price. There is a constant fear. In the need to understand the fear so it can be controlled, there is the urgent desire to learn about what is happening. But we have had nowhere to turn.

Why are we afraid?

Often, throughout my life, I have been awakened by some figure standing at my bedside. Although these visits were comforting visions when I was small, as an adult I find them quite disturbing and often jolt awake, screaming. I seem to have acquired a "fear of the unexplainable" and find I am afraid to let the spirits help me and afraid to ask how I can help them. Each time they appear in the middle of the night, I am startled awake, frightened and caught off-guard. Despite my earnest efforts to keep my head and do better the next time, I am still unable to think clearly or to react quickly enough to even ask them why they have appeared.

Recently, after much meditation and introspection on this dilemma, I have concluded that although I am now not as receptive to nighttime spirit visits as when I was a child, I do, now as an adult, understand their messages better. I am proud to have come such a long way by myself in understanding my gift and its purpose.

So with introspection and analysis, comes a better understanding of the fear. Perhaps this understanding will give me better control of my fear.

I can only track the gift in my family to a certain point, after which, the trail goes cold. My closest source for this research has been my mother and other older family members, but as people age, their memories fade. While growing up, these "gifted" family members were taught, as are a lot of people still today that the unusual things they had experienced were not normal and they were constantly discouraged from speaking of them. Because of this suppression and the frailties of her advancing age, I am only able to get disjointed memory fragments from Mom these days.

I have been interested in this gift for as long as I can remember and try not to take it for granted for one minute. This ability has always made me feel special and unique. I have found the spirits can break up a pretty boring routine of going to work every day!

I have experienced some pretty exciting things, and have heard from other family members and even from my customers about some pretty interesting stuff! They are all different people with different lifestyles, yet all have had very similar experiences. It causes one to wonder if the line of separation between this world and the next is really just a "fine veil."

How can so many people who are having such similar experiences and relating to similar situations be so wrong? Could these just be dreams? Can such a wide variety of people really have the same dream? How is it possible for a five year old to remember every little "dream" from such a young age into adulthood and with such clarity?

Although there are many fad theories on "spirit" type dreams currently accepted by the medical profession, for me, the dream theory just doesn't hold up to the light of my experiences. We'll just throw that dream right out the window.

I have said previously that this book is spirit guided. Spirits want only for their stories to be heard. Through my self-realization and eventual acceptance of my gift, I have truly come to believe that my experiences are meant to be read by others for the purpose of education; to let others who are experiencing the same visions will know that they are not alone. And also, to help those spirits who have something yet left to say or do for those loved ones they have left behind.

Their visits have a reason. Although frightened and trying to avoid and ignore the spirit visits at first, I now try to figure them out. It is like a puzzle and each time they bless me with a visit, I become more in tune and more on track.

I hope to one day be skillful enough to be able to pass on spirit messages to others, anytime anywhere, for free. I think that's the purpose of the gift. Right now I am just learning and enjoying every event.

I some times go weeks or months without a vision, but I want you to know that doesn't mean that the visions are over or that the spirits are gone. They may just have nothing to say for a while. This gift is the one thing that makes me unique and has sent me on a path of exploring and discovery.

Because of this gift and a message received one night, I opened my New Age store. I tried doing it the traditional way that most start a business, but I couldn't get any funding. So I paid for the store front out of the sales from my popular and profitable web page.

In retrospect, I wouldn't trade any experience for the world. Each situation as you will read, relates to different events forth coming in my life or those around me. Some I don't clearly understand, but as time goes on, I sort them through.

I wish that I could say that by seeing spirits you can make better choices in your life, or that the spirits can help you hit the lottery. But it doesn't work that way, or should I say, they haven't done that yet for me. For me, the purpose of their visits has to relay helpful information for a specific person about a specific event.

I think it's all about self-discovery and self-acceptance.

As we all know, these types of gifts are usually not acknowledged in a positive manner. The twelve-year-old daughter of a friend of mine had been seeing spirits for a while. My friend recently spoke with me about her daughter, concerned, because she is an honor roll student, has never been in any kind of trouble, under any type of family stress, yet lately, has repeatedly been telling her parents she "sees ghosts."

Understandably upset, my friend and her husband stopped into my store before they took her to a doctor for a psychological evaluation. I talked at length with them both until closing time that night and after some questioning about her family's history, we discovered that my friend's mother and grandmother also had seen spirits in their lifetimes.

Although, a little less distressed after our conversation ended, my friend was still hesitant to accept that the spirits her daughter was seeing were not just figments of an overactive teenage imagination.

My store had engaged a talented psychic to read a group of people at one time, so my friend and her husband both booked a seat for this reading. They felt that in order to help their daughter, if she was truly seeing spirits, they should begin to learn more about such things.

The structure of our world is based on our beliefs passed down to us in our upbringing. It is disturbing, I know, to watch fragile realities shatter when confronted with the possibility of the existence of alternate realities, which defy conventional explanation.

We have all been raised with many "traditional" and cultural beliefs, which have remained with us through to adulthood. Many of us have grown old, carrying the unspoken secret of our "spirit visits" and "visions" with us, not being able to talk to anyone about such "dark" things for fear people would think we were crazy and rush to lock us away or because we ourselves were not ready to deal with them as they occurred in our lives.

I have been most fortunate while growing up, to have been able to talk to my mother, brothers, sister, my husband and my two daughters about these events. Even though the events I recount often cause concern to my daughters, they sometimes get brave and ask for more information.

"How did we get this way?" they asked.

"We were just born this way," I told them.

It never once occurred to me to consider what I saw then and am still seeing now as "not right" or that I should seek help for some mental instability.

For those who experience the same things, this book is for you.

You are not alone.

Chapter Two

Spirits in the Light

Spirits do not just come to me at night or in through messages in my dreams. There has been a time when I have just walked past someone and glimpsed a shadowy figure behind him or her, or have actually seen an entire ghostly figure and have done a double take, because it looked just like a person in complete detail.

I have also experienced orbs, which are spheres of light or energy. These orbs can show up in photographs (not the uniformly round blobs attributed to dust particles) or as a flash in corner of your eye as you are looking at something. To me, the orbs and shadowy figures have become "spirits in the light."

One daytime vision incident in particular, stands out in my mind.   I had been employed in a small office a few years ago, as an accounts receivable manager. A co-worker had just returned from vacation, or so I thought. As I passed his office on his first day back, I saw an elderly gentleman leaning over his shoulder looking down at his work. Since we were friends, I knew I could talk to this co-worker about what I had seen.

I leaned in his office said, "You have a guy standing behind you! He looks like the 'fried chicken' guy," meaning a certain Colonel of southern fried chicken fame.

Of course, when you say something like that to someone, they're not going to let you just keep on walking! He called me back into his office and asked why I'd said that. I told him again what I saw and then added that he wanted me to "let you know."

The vision was of an older gentleman, dressed circa Civil War style. He had a long narrow face, white hair and beard. I didn't know the connection, and didn't think get an "impression" that he and my co-worker were related.

The co-worker then confessed to me that in fact he had *not* been on vacation, but instead had just returned from his father's funeral. He and his family laid his father to rest in an old cemetery in an old-fashioned manner. He told me that because the graveyard was so old and crowded, that they had very little room to move around. As they placed his father into the ground, he had stepped on the next grave. He had felt very guilty for doing this and thought that may have been when he had possibly made a connection with the spirit. I actually thought that this spirit went back a lot farther in time, but I did not want to explain why I got the impression that this might have been a relative, or some deep connection from the past. The main thing was that the spirit only wanted my co-worker to know he was with him.

This was not the only spirit vision that I had at this place of employment. I was working in my office one afternoon, when the owner's Stepfather stopped in to say hello. He was like a Dad to us all; we all laughed and got along very well. He was a man of many friends, some of whom were in the government and even the police force. He had recently survived one bout of cancer, and we all really thought that he had beaten it. On that day, however, he began to tell me how his cancer had returned.

As I looked at him, while he spoke of some upcoming testing, my focus on his face turned fuzzy and then went gray. The next thing I knew, I was standing at my father's viewing, looking at Dad in the same church, filled with the same faces that were there then; as if I had momentarily gone back in time, but I could still the owner's Stepfather speaking to me in "real time." Then just as quickly, it was over. I blinked and I was back, looking at this kind gentleman's gray face with worry in his eyes. My heart became heavy, for I knew what sadness this vision foretold. I could not tell his daughter; it's just not something you mention. He did pass a few months later of cancer. We all miss him dearly.

Later, I talked about this experience with my family and some close friends to understand why I had a vision in this manner. The owner's Stepfather was not related to my father or me, so why my father was's viewing used to warn me of this gentleman's impending death? My friends felt that one connecting tie between my father and him, was the cancer; another connection was that his daughter was a very dear friend of mine, making it a 'fatherly' one.

I don't know why I flashed back to a similar time. It truly felt as if I was physically present in another place and time. It seemed nobody could see me or even knew I was there. I could still hear him

26

speaking as I returned to the current situation and had heard all that he said; never missing a beat. The consensus of my family and friends about that experience was, that I was probably momentarily in two places at once. How weird.

It seems that Kelly, one of my closest friends, one of those friends you can talk to about anything too, has had some weird experiences.

Kelly told me that one of her friends was recently killed in an ATV accident. She, her friend and her friend's son all went to the funeral. When they returned to Kelly's house, the friend's son asked if he could get something to drink and went off into the kitchen. Suddenly, he rushed into the living room, pale white and shaken, saying that he had just seen "the dead guy from the funeral" at the kitchen table putting on his boots. He nervously described how "the dead guy" just tilted his head and looked at him. Everyone immediately went into the kitchen to see, but Kelly's friend was gone. Kelly and I felt that he probably just wanted to say good-bye and to let everyone in the house know that he was ok. The boy who saw him was thirteen at the time and never had anything similar happen until that date.

I have also had surprise "visits" at my house. One night, after coming home from foster parent training, my husband and I walked into our house and turned on the lights, as we all do. I walked across the kitchen toward the hallway and as I neared the entry between the kitchen and the one living room, I could see a girl sitting in my rocking chair that was next to our fireplace, she rocked it slowly back and forth.

She was wearing a light blue terrycloth bathrobe and was dripping wet, and as if she had just gotten out of the shower or worse yet, a thought raced thru my head, dripping wet as if she had drowned! It gave me such a helpless feeling. Her eyes were blackened and it seemed to me she that looked angry. Strong impressions of overdose, suicide or foul play hit me like a brick as she continued to stare, looking up to me with her head cocked to the side. I stood still, unable to move.

I felt a heavy sadness and I knew that she wanted me to help her with something left unfinished. I felt as if she was pushed to this point of contacting me, that she had no other recourse for closure. If

27

her death was suicide or a drowning, then someone else was behind it. It seemed she was there for quite a while; she was not worried about me seeing her or telling anyone else that she was there. She was angered and she wanted me to know it.

My husband noticed me standing, frozen in place and staring at the chair. He asked what was wrong and I told him there was a girl sitting in my chair. He immediately walked over to what appeared to him to be an empty chair, but said it was freezing cold there. The little girl vanished from the chair as I spoke and within minutes, the surrounding temperature returned to normal.

It was at that point that I realized that my visions were changing; I was now seeing people both in daytime and nighttime, whether I was awake or asleep. I was growing in a way that I could not explain, but I actually enjoyed seeing them like this, more than having them startle me while trying to fall asleep.

I still see her as clearly in my mind now, as I did on that night. I often find myself thinking of this girl. Although I didn't know her personally, I now believe, based on information which reached me years later, that she had been a friends, friends daughter who had committed suicide. Although I could not hear her message, I certainly felt her deep sorrow.

I did not approach her parents with this vision of their daughter because I did not want to re-open painful memories. And although I felt strongly that I was right, interpreting spirit messages was new to me and I just didn't trust the timing or myself. I was afraid that if I were wrong; they would be quite offended that a total stranger would dare bring up such a private subject. There was quite a good chance they would think I was crazy.

My home is along the Lake Erie shoreline. Because of this, I thought that the vision could have also been from a girl who had drowned. Perhaps I had "picked" her up when walking along my property there, or maybe she died from some altogether different method. I had been working long hours and was just not on top of the latest local events. All rationalizations aside, how her clothing looked and the strong feelings I got from her, still made me look at this as a suicide occurring in the house or bathroom area. One thing I can surely tell you, she is still angry.

The next day, I went to my chair and sat there where she had appeared. I was still able to sense sadness around me. After a little while, I rose from the chair, still debating whether to approach the parents about this incident. But common sense quickly won that argument and I remained silent. Fearful of being wrong or thought crazy, I continued the silence; many years have now passed. If it was something unresolved, I regret that I could not help her with closure, but my belief is that all things work themselves out, and the truth will eventually be known.

Although the visions have felt like some sort of a gift, their purpose was all too often, unclear. As mentioned before, I had noticed that my visions were changing. Also, I realized that once I had a vision, I began to dream about the person or people from my vision, shortly thereafter.

I truly believe that these visions are the result of someone trying to communicate with me, to get a message "across worlds." Perhaps they choose to appear to me only because I am one of the few who are able to see them. The thought has occurred to me that if I could communicate a step further with them, maybe I could help them and give them peace at last.

Whether you choose to believe it or not, everyone has spirit guides, or guardians. These guides are always trying to communicate with you in one way or another, through dreams or other senses. But once they know you are open to them visually, you often receive some guardians who just drop in to hang out!

I was lying on the couch one night as my husband, Bill, watched T.V, when out of the corner of my eye, I saw a tall, slender, elderly man.

"Bill, you have someone leaning over your shoulder," I told him and then described the gentleman.

My husband immediately recognized the description as his "Grandpop" George, who was his father's father. Grand pop George had hardly ever seen Bill growing up. He didn't seem to care about his grandchildren in his life here on earth, but he was with him now and I was "told" to make sure my husband knew it. They both shared the love of fishing and this is possibly why Grandpop George had become Bill's spirit guide.

If anything, I think that these spirit people just want to let you know they are present.

By not spending time with his grand children, Grandpop George had missed out on a lot, but he was making up for it now. When told about this incident, my husband's father simply stated that since Grandpop George "never wanted to acknowledge you kids when he was alive," he most certainly wouldn't be watching over Bill now.

I disagree based on my experiences so far with spirit guides. It appears that mistakes made during one's physical life, do not necessarily prevent one's spirit from being a part of another life after death. As spirit guides, these spirits have received a second chance to make a positive difference in someone else's life.

Recently on July 3rd, 2004, my mother, two of my brothers, Rusty and Chuck, my husband Bill, my daughter and I all went to visit my father's grave in New Jersey. As I stood at his gravesite with my brothers, nostalgic memories of our old blue house flashed into my head. I vividly recalled the parties when I use to come home every year, when the driveway full of cars from my brothers and their friends, who were all of driving age; we all had gone to school together. I though it was weird how years of memories can flood your mind in seconds. A wave of sadness washed over me. Those days were completely gone forever.

My mind whirled as I thought about Dad. He never got a chance to retire, never got to come to see my house in Pennsylvania. He had planned to come up to spend Thanksgiving with us in 2002, but died October 19th that year. He lived a very stressful life, cursed with financial stress, but he did manage to keep a roof over our heads. No, we didn't have money, or even "normal" things that are now taken for granted, but we did have a happy home. I was sad that he did not realize all his dreams, but proud of him for working so hard for us.

We each ended our silent prayers and walked together thru the graveyard toward the flagpole and the wall of names of the many WWI and WWII veterans, who had made the ultimate sacrifice to keep us free.

As we made our way to the half waypoint, in the warm, humid New Jersey weather, a sudden flood of goose bumps kicked up along my left side. My left leg, left arm and left side of my face all developed big goose bumps. When I commented on them to my family, everyone took turns curiously inspecting them. Now, we all know there is no way you can turn goose bumps on and off, especially on just one side of your body!

I know that this weird occurrence was Father's way of letting us know he was aware of us being there. Because I had been feeling guilty about only getting a chance to visit his grave yearly, I felt he used my goose-bumps as a way of getting my attention, to acknowledge our visit; and that he was glad we had come. We took some pictures around this time and I hope to insert one of them in this, or a future book.

Just so you don't think I get the goose bumps every time I go into a graveyard, let me tell you of another special graveyard visit we made that week.

On the following Monday after visiting Dad's gravesite, we went to Salem, MA and walked thru one of the old cemeteries there, just to look at the inscriptions on the older hand-carved headstones. While there, I did not get any rush of goose bumps at all; just an overall sad feeling. We then went to the infamous Salem, MA burial ground; again, no goose bumps. But I was not surprised to discover afterward, that the many pictures we developed from our two cameras had "orbs" and a few other interesting surprises!

I showed these interesting vacation pictures to others when I returned. They were quite a conversation piece, and steered the topic into "things seen but not often discussed." It seemed that once I decided to open up to my family and friends about my ability, I discovered that "seeing spirits" is actually not so unusual.

For example, my friend Connie once told me about a time she had gone downstairs (in her house) to get her son a bottle from the refrigerator, and when she looked to the left of the sink, she saw a vision standing there. Although, when she described it to me it seemed more like an alien than a human, I do believe that he was a spirit guide. She told me that she just went about her business that night and didn't think anything of it till the next day.

When spirits come to me, they appear in their human form standing, or sitting, as if they were alive. But others may see spirits differently, like Connie. My mother sees the figures floating.

Mom had a stroke a few years back and was recovering at the hospital, when one day, a young lady who was having an asthma attack, was brought in. The nurses set her up in the bed next to Mom. Mom watched her through a little opening in the curtain, as they tried to calm the girl and gave her an injection to help ease her breathing.

But something went wrong; the shot backfired for some reason.

A sudden flurry of nurses rushed into the little space around the girl's bed. Each nurse, without panicking but with urgent concentration, did his or her job. Mom was in the first bed by the door and could clearly see the nurses as they entered the room. But when she saw a figure float calmly into that area, Mom got worried and quickly shut her eyes so the figure would not see her watching. At this point, Mom listened as one of the nurses came over to see if she was sleeping. She peeked as the nurse walked away.

When she thought it was safe and that the figure had finally floated past her, Mom opened her eyes. She watched the girl, now lying down on the bed, flop, rise up once with a gasp and then flop down a second time. That was all, and she passed on. Mom believes that they gave her the wrong medicine in that injection.

I know from unfortunate personal experience, that medical mistakes can happen.

When I was in fifth grade, Doctors in a local emergency room gave me a shot because I was having an asthma attack. I remember clearly hearing them yelling at someone else in the room, saying they "gave me enough for a full grown man!" I weighed eighty pounds at that time; that night was a long one at the hospital. Mom said my lips had turned blue and there was an odd bluish tinge over my whole body. All I remember of that night, was that I felt like I was speeding, but at least I could finally breathe!

Years later, when I mentioned this "floating figure" experience of Mom's to a friend, who was also a little gifted, he told me an interesting theory.

He theorized that the floating figure Mom saw was a "collector of souls." I had never heard of this before. Indeed, he said, to see one was a true gift and she was very lucky to have the ability to see such spirits. When the young lady rose up off the bed twice, he said it was because she had two souls and each time the collector took one of her souls, she flopped up off the bed. The floating figure did not kill her; she was already dead at this point.

This theory makes as much sense as any other I have heard. It is believable to me that she was a special person and possessed two souls. I have no personal experience with witnessing something like this, but Mom has seen spirits her entire life, and this was just another vision to her.

The closest experience I have regarding the two-soul theory is one that was relayed to me as a way to explain what I see when I close my eyes. I see a set of eyes on a face looking back at me. I have been told that is my twin soul. Although not many people have them, it's not entirely uncommon.

Chapter Three

Spirits in the Night

This chapter introduces some specific events, which have occurred involving me and some of my family members; events, which happened when we were all tucked away, supposedly safe and sound, in our beds at night.

Usually, when I see spirits or visions, it's in a rest state; that period in-between being awake and being asleep, when I have just gotten comfortable, and am thinking I will soon be out like a light. I wonder what prompts me to pop open my eyes to find someone standing beside my bed. What triggers my mind to the vision?

Recently one night, in that half-awake, half-asleep limbo, a vision came to me of a little African American girl. She seemed approximately three years old and was wearing nothing but a dirty, cloth diaper, which sagged heavily from her frail body. Her eyes were large, dark and brimmed with tears. A tear welled and rolled down her dirty cheek; her one hand wiped it away and the other hand reached out for me. I had just begun to reach for her, when suddenly a large white man appeared behind her. His hand slammed down on her shoulder with such force that I screamed out at the top of my lungs. *He killed her, he killed her*, was all that raced through my mind! He was angered by her crying and had used his brute force to hush her.

I believe that this blow ended this little girl's life and that's why she appeared to me in vision form.

Although still I don't know what the vision meant, I have analyzed why I saw it; what I saw was crystal clear. I believe that she was looking for comfort and help. To help give her final peace, she just needed someone to know what had happened to her and I was receptive. As far as the white man, I have no ideas about him and am unable to help him. In addition, I have not been able to place the geography of this vision. Perhaps it is connected to the land around my home, through one of the land's previous owners or residents. To me, the shortness of her sad life and method of this little girl's death is an unthinkable tragedy.

I sometimes wonder if it was this particular vision, which awaked my awareness to the plight of neglected and unwanted children, because shortly thereafter, I became a foster parent. Most of the children who were in my foster care, had been abused and neglected. (I don't believe in all of the foster agency's programs, but if you ever have the chance to share your home and be a foster parent, please do!) The experience of foster parenting has greatly enriched my life!

As mentioned in previous chapters, I had opened my retail store in February of 2003. I am proud, still today, that I did it all; did everything without any bank financing, or by any partnership. No one was interested in giving me a loan to open a "new age" store anyway. It's not a common, everyday business in most towns. I did not sell anything of questionable nature, but I did have some pretty "witchy" type items that were unique.

The store, Cindy's Eye of the Moon, was open most of the week, thanks to the many hours of work by my two wonderful volunteers. Sadly, on May 28th, 2004, I reluctantly closed my store due to irreconcilable differences with the new owner of the store plaza.

Before closing the store, I had hosted some awesome spiritual photography classes there. I also had some wonderful physic events, involving renowned physics and readers. Directly resulting from the insights gained from those events, I impulsively decided as I closed up one night, to leave a cassette tape recording; running throughout the night, hoping to capture sounds or messages from any spirits.

I closed the door to my office. As I closed the bead curtain in the back room, I received a clear, urgent message in my mind, *just hang out a little longer at the store*. I shook it off and thought, *it's time to go home, now!*

The bead curtain clacked loudly as it beat against the door for a few minutes after it closed. I waited for it to finish its noise and listened from inside the store to see if there were any sounds coming from elsewhere in the plaza. I wanted no sounds to interfere with the night's recording experiment.

Satisfied the recording would be "clean," I locked the store up securely for the night. I remember walking to my car, it was still light out yet, but I had this anxious, odd feeling that I needed to be careful. I pulled out of the store parking lot, and looked in my rearview mirror. All seemed in order; nothing appeared unusual. As I made my next turn, I saw a car I recognized as belonging to a teenager who frequented the house next door to the store. (I have had run-ins with him in the past, for harassing my customers. No matter how nicely he was asked to respect others, he pretty much did everything he could to scare my customers, and bother me.)

The car, with this unpleasant young man and a crew of his rowdy friends, followed me as I headed for home. I randomly turned into a parking lot, hoping that they would just pass me by. I was afraid if they followed me home and found out where I lived, that this kid would cause the same harassment problems at my house.

It was dark by this time. I had been watching for them to pass by the parking lot, but decided, after a few more minutes of waiting, that I must have missed them in the darkness. It seemed safe, so I pulled back out on to the main road. From the rear of the same parking lot, they pulled out onto the main road, right behind me. My hands shook as I picked up my cell phone to call my friend whose husband was a Police Officer.

I swung back around and into another section of the same parking lot and they also turned into this section. This time, parked really close to me, as if trying to block me in. My friend was now on the phone and I alerted her to what was happening, in case the situation turned bad. The kids in the car stared directly at me as I talked on the phone. I quickly pulled out from the parking lot one more time, but this time they did not follow me. Still shaken, I headed home.

When I walked in the front door at home, I called the police and filed an incident report.

(A few days later the, the same kid took a severed deer head into the yard of the house next door and nailed it to a tree, which faced my store's rear parking lot, as if to scare off my customers. The rest of the deer's body was tossed out and left to rot beside the house. The customers had to walk by the rotting carcass in order to get to the store's front door. I reported this continuing problem of my customer's harassment to the store plaza's original landlord. The situation was eventually corrected.)

I opened my store the next day without incident. But when I listened to the tape, about ten minutes into the recording of the previous night, the "chills" hit me.

Clearly heard over and over again, a voice on the tape whispered, "Come back. Come back Cindy. Come back!"

It seemed I was actually being warned not to leave the store. But even though I did leave, I somehow knew that night to watch for someone following me.

I had let a few people listen to the recording throughout the day as they stopped in to visit. They all confirmed they heard same thing, clearly. (I know I still have that tape somewhere, but I haven't been able to locate it since I closed and packed up the store.)

Had I ignored the voices in my mind, I would have just driven home as usual; innocently leading those troublemaking kids right my house. Who knows how long they could have played head games with me! My spirit guides alerted me, and I listened to them and tried to protect myself. It was comforting to know that spirits were with me in the store.

After shutting the store down, my visions stopped for a while; I'm not sure why. Then, one night at home, I saw a shadow standing near my bed. This was the first spirit to come to me in a long time.

The message was undoubtedly clear in my mind and was specifically for me alone. The spirit was letting me know that everything was going to be OK. Although I may not be able to see what is in front of me, he assured me that they (the spirits) were here to help me and guide me whenever needed. (For a few days after this visitation, my husband complained of sore ribs. I had bruised him while frightened by pushing myself away from the shadow figure and into him that night.)

It was a Sunday night when I awoke screaming at the next visitation. This time I saw two girls, one taller than the other, standing by my side of the bed. I thought back to the three girls that I had seen years before, near the time of my father's passing and wondered why I only saw two girls this time. I shook my husband to wake him.

"I have two girls standing by my side of the bed," I told him.

He sleepily said, "That's OK, I have one on this side too."

We seemed to think nothing of it and both went back to sleep.

He has occasionally seen a few things, but to have the both of us see the same spirit together, was truly unusual and had never happened before. I don't yet know the reason for their appearance, but I can say that I was actually happy to see them again. (The next morning, my daughters reported they had heard my screaming that night from their room. My younger daughter told the older daughter to "go see what Mom is screaming at," but the older refused with a "no way!")

After some thought, I decided the two girls standing by my side of the bed represented my two daughters.

At the time, my oldest daughter Tabitha was home on military leave and had made plans to visit her grandfather's grave for the first time. She had been stationed overseas when he passed away and had been unable to attend his funeral at that time. When she was home on her next leave, we made plans to take her to see my father's grave. But our plans didn't work out that way. At the very time we were scheduled to make the trip to my father's grave, Tabitha instead, ended up visiting her grandmother, whose frail health had taken a turn for the worse.

This brings me to the explanation of the one girl standing by my husband's side of the bed. To me, the one girl standing alone was a symbolic representation of "being separate." She gave me the impression that I was being advised that everyone was not going to be "together" during that family visit.

As noted before, I am not the only family member that has had visions.

My nephew, Derrick, also sees them; and they frighten him.

On August 3, 2004, Derrick was staying overnight at an apartment shared by Mom and my sisters. A diabetic, Mom's blood sugar had been unstable and often unexpectedly dropped low. Because of the dangers inherent in a low blood sugar attack, my sister made sure someone stayed with Mom while she was at work and arranged for visiting nurses and various family members to come in.

This particular night, my nephew was staying with Mom. It was late, he said, and Mom was asleep on the couch, when he looked up from the TV to see my father, a man in a military uniform, a young boy and a dog, all standing near Mom's bedroom door.

Seeing the spirit of his grandfather again, scared him so much, his heart raced uncontrollably. He began noisily gasping for breath and startled my mother awake. When she looked over at him to see what was wrong, she thought he was having a stroke! The vision had scared him so much he could not sleep the rest of the night. When my sister returned home from work the next morning, Derrick was still shaking from fear.

To identify the other individual spirits in Derrick's vision requires some family background, so here goes.

Father's Dad was German with the last name of Spickenreuther. I had always wanted to know more about my relatives in Germany, but not much was known of our family history, just because our family didn't talk much. I do know that my grandfather had two brothers, both of whom were in WWII and both had been POWs. Family thought that at the end of the war, one brother had gone back to Germany to help rebuild his country and the other had stayed in the USA and settled in Arizona. My relatives told me that Grandfather didn't keep in touch with his brothers and the contact was lost after the war.

The family history of the brothers separated by WWI is the reason I came to identify the spirit Derrick saw standing in the uniform, as my grandfather's brother. (Presently, I am not sure who the younger boy and dog are. Interestingly, my Nephew says that all of his visions contain a dog. The dog may be something symbolic for him to figure out later in life.)

Derrick does not want to see these spirits any more and gets a little frustrated with them. I hope in time he will learn to accept them and to enjoy sharing his stories for others to hear.

My brother Chuck had a similar experience on the very same night as Derrick.

Chuck told me that it was about 3:30 a.m. and he was watching TV; he was again unable to sleep because of his chronic back pain. He heard his bedroom door squeak open but didn't think too much of it. He heard a few footsteps and when they stopped by the refrigerator, he assumed it was his wife getting a drink. But when he didn't hear anything else, he got up to investigate and saw his bedroom door was closed. He opened the door to ask his wife if everything was OK. She was snoring loudly and had obviously been asleep the whole time!

He dismissed the incident until I telephoned to tell him about Derrick seeing Dad and the other spirits. So now all three of us have seen, heard, and felt my father. He wants to get our attention. Let's just say we hear you, Dad!

The next day, coming home from work, I took a different route home and drove very carefully, just in case Dad's appearance had been a warning; he may have been trying to alert me to something. But the drive home was without incident. (As I told you in the beginning, this book is spirit driven, so these little signs are to alert me, but also to make me note them.)

If nothing else, I recently told my husband, when I get old and the Doctors are wondering if I am mentally impaired because I "see spirits," because I have written this book, I will have a documented life-long history of being connected with "paranormal events."

It was Mother's birthday on that day, and the thought occurred to me that Dad may have been appearing to all of us because of her birthday, but my gut feeling was that was medically related.

Father passed away in his sleep and now Mom is afraid to go to sleep. She is also afraid of seeing spirits now. She is afraid she will see the collector of souls coming for hers. At one time in her life, she didn't find them frightening, but now as the years take their toll on her health and the reality of her impending mortality becomes apparent, I think she does.

I have come to terms with them, and yes, they can be frightening as they appear in the wildest places, but their messages are worth hearing

On August 16th, 2004, I was almost asleep when, I saw an older gentleman with mussed white hair standing by my dresser, wearing an old-style prisoner jail uniform with black and white stripes. He seemed to be covered in some sort of white dirt, or dust, as if he had been working on rock piles. It was just a quick vision and no feelings or other impressions were felt.

The next night, August 17th, I had three visitors at different times throughout the night. These spirits were *really* trying to get my attention! Needless to say, our house didn't get much sleep that night because they startled me, and I awoke screaming, each time.

By the third vision, I was very irritable at being disturbed so many times.

"Darn people!" I yelled at them. "Leave me alone!"

I was just so tired I couldn't think straight.

Only the last vision, can I remember clearly enough to describe. Maybe that's why they persisted; they were determined to get me to remember their visits. This last visitor was a man with long hair, a long white robe and was holding a small brown animal. While the spirits succeeded in getting me to remember the vision, that's all I saw and there was no meaning connected with it.

With little sleep the night before, the next day at work developed into a *very* long day. When it was finally quitting time, I readied for the long drive home. Because of my fatigue, I knew my driving reaction time would be off and I would need to drive with extreme care. So I decided to take a slow route home, and had planed to make a right turn when I got to the traffic light. Suddenly, at the intersection in front of me, I watched as two cars nearly missed a head-on collision with each other; horns blew and tires screeched loudly to a stop. I was not worried though. I slowly tapped my brakes as they got their vehicles under control and stayed a short distance away from them.

Then it happened! The car behind me hit me, and hit hard enough to shake me. The impact caused my car to jump into neutral. The other driver and I both pulled our cars over to the side of the road to inspect the damage. Amazingly, we found that there were just a few scratches and exchanged insurance information. But by the time I got home, my back had begun to hurt, and my neck had gotten quite stiff. Since I had just recovered from back surgery a year prior, I knew all the signs of accident-related back problems.

Immediately after the accident, it "clicked" in my head. _This was the reason for all the spirits coming to me,_ I thought to myself. They just wanted me to be careful! Needless to say, the back pain did disappear after a few weeks.

My brother, Chuck, had an unusual event happen in September 2004, one of his most recent. He said he was lying in bed one night and awoke because he felt something on his chest. He looked down to his chest to see a young girl lying on his chest.

She looked up at him and in a very dark voice said, "Come with me!"

Startled at seeing her and hearing her ominous tone, he flailed his arms, punching at the vision. She spoke again, now trying a more welcoming tone, but he said you could clearly hear a lot of static in her voice. No spirit had ever spoken like that to him before, and when he told me of this incident, I felt that this spirit was not one to be taken lightly.

She did not seem to fit in with any of the ones I have experienced. Perhaps she was warning him to be careful of someone who would be trying to seduce him by trying to talk him into something that is not good for him. This whole thing caused him to feel extremely unsettled or "freaked out," in his terms.

To cleanse his house of any lingering negativity from this spirit, I mailed my brother Chuck some sage for him to burn for ritual purification. He burned the sage as instructed, yet despite this, a few nights later he had a similar experience. This time there were two spirits, and they held him down on his bed. He explained, they did not allow him to move as they called for him to come with them

I was concerned at this point, that he somehow had attracted something negative. Or these spirits were trying unusually hard to get his attention. I was thinking of this situation as I drove to work the next day, and it finally dawned on me that Chuck was being warned, that "things were not as wonderful as they seemed."

When I called my brother that evening and told him of my interpretation of his visitations, he told me in the same conversation, that he was going to accept a settlement on an injury case that has burdened him for many years. I told him that the spirit is telling him to be careful that things (pertaining to this settlement) may not be as perfect as they appear.

A few days passed and I called him again. He told me had "signed off" on the settlement. When he informed me of the particulars of his settlement, it seemed to me that he did not get nearly as much as he should have, since his injury resulted in two surgeries. But he said was comfortable with the arrangements and had been very careful to read everything he signed, questioning many items. They had gone before the Judge who looked over the paperwork and signed "in agreement" of the settlement amount.

A few weeks later, my brother received a letter from his lawyer stating that his office had made an error in calculating the figures submitted for the settlement amount; the actual settlement amount was $20,000.00 less than the amount declared on the agreement which the Judge had signed. All the figures itemized on the settlement papers were correct, just the total amount was wrong. Whether a type-o or miscalculation, the result was that my brother was short by $20,000 on his injury settlement. He was, understandably, very upset over this. The settlement amount now wouldn't even cover his medical expenses, yet alone his suffering.

The spirits wanted to get his attention. They truly tried and did very a commendable job at communication. I regret that we were not able to be more precise with the interpretation so that he would have better known what to look for. I often think of him.

I know he and I will both pay a lot more attention to our messengers.

Chapter Four

The Path

On a recent weekend afternoon, while settling in for a nap, I was nearly asleep, when a vision of a man appeared in the room. He whispered that he wanted to take me to show me the secrets of the fairies. I felt myself floating up, weightless, like astral travel, a form of leaving your body without waking up. I became frightened; I did not trust this guy and forced myself awake.

I regret now that I was not brave enough to go with him. I am very interested in magic, mystical, and spiritual things; fairies just happen to be one of those. However, I do not agree with everything written on the subject. I often wonder what he had been ready to show me and realize I missed an opportunity that will probably never come again. At that time, I realized need better control of my fears and vowed to learn ways of self control and self comfort.

For the last few years, I have felt my grandmother around me. I felt her presence guiding me through the opening of my store. But when Father passed away in October 2002, she went to Mom, who needed her badly while she endured a terrible financial ordeal caused my father's life insurance.

Father had worked at a casino in Atlantic City. Because of a loophole in the policy's language, the casino stated he was not eligible for his life insurance until October 20, 2002. Father passed away 2 hours short; 10:00 p.m. in the evening of October 19, 2002. The casino's administration did not budge, and the insurance was not awarded to Mother after Dad's death. The lack of this insurance, while only a meager $10,000, caused extreme financial hardship on Mother; she had to sell her house to pay for Father's funeral expenses. She was heartsick about the decision. That is why my grandmother's spirit went to comfort her. (After the sale of her house, Mom lived with my sister for a few years and now lives with me.)

As I said previously, during her life, Grandmother also showed a little of the gift. She could sense death the in same way as my mother and I could, with our "field of purple flowers."

When I had the "purple flowers" experience about six months before my father died, I told my brothers and sisters to prepare, and let Mom know to make plans of her own too. There was a short time when Dad seemed to have beaten the cancer, but his last treatment cost him dearly. I remember walking into his hospital room in New Jersey for a visit and feeling a sudden feeling a rush of oppressive heat; so choking that I moved across the room to be free of it. I mentioned nothing of it, thinking that the hospital's heating was probably out of order.

I sat behind Dad and watched as he pointed twice to the same spot in the room and called out to Mom, "Hey Anita, look who it is!"

"There's no one there," Mom said.

But I told Mom to let him talk; I wanted to know who was there, because I too had felt someone else's presence in the room.

The feeling of this presence was not cold, like when visions would appear in my house, or when I would walk near someone who had a spirit with them. This feeling was hot and made me feel sick; an entirely new association with a spirit. That last day, I didn't get to stay with Dad as long as I would have liked. Because I had to travel back to Pennsylvania for work the next day, I had to cut our visit short. I will never forget the anxiety; I didn't want to leave. I knew there would be no coming back to see Dad again. I knew this would be the last time I saw him.

The next day, back at home in Pennsylvania, I was in my shipping room, packing up some orders for my store. The phone rang; it was my brother saying he was going to bring Dad home now because Dad just didn't want to be in the hospital any more. I agreed and said to go ahead.

As I hung up from my brother's call, my husband came in the room and complained about all lights in the house flickering like crazy.

"Who called?" he asked me.

I told him, and added, "But it's too late. Dad has already passed on."

I left my shipping room to go my computer and the lights started flickering again. There had been no storms or unusual winds outside that night. The flickering lights were just Dad's final good-bye. We received the "official" call of his death approximately three hours later.

My father's first appearance as a spirit was to my youngest daughter. She was very scared, but I explained that he was just looking after her. A few days after his visit, she broke her arm. I think he visited her to warn her to be a little more careful in basketball tryouts.

My brother and I wondered when he would appear in physical form to one of us. To date, he has not yet done that, but he has also appeared to my nephew, Derrick, on a few occasions.

The first visit Dad made to Derrick, he appeared and stood in front of him and said, "Help her."

The next day, I got a call from my nephew asking me if I knew what "help her" meant.

I had him describe the surroundings in the vision. He said he was at his grandmother's house.

"I would say he wants you to help your grandmother," I said. "Perhaps she needs something done, or will be needing assistance soon, and he wants you to be there to help her out."

Derrick didn't say much, just "OK."

When I told Mom of Dad's visit to my nephew, Mom said, "Why would he be so caring like that now? He was not like that when he was alive!"

I surmised that even though Dad had a hard time showing any feelings and often communicated with a lot of yelling in this world, in the next world he was now free of things which caused him hardship and he finally seemed happy. The stresses of life can cause us all to show our ugly sides.

In addition to seeing my father, Derrick has also seen a little girl who had passed away from his school. She just appeared in front of him one day, and that was it. He was petty surprised and we never did figure out what that visit meant. Maybe she just wanted to relay a message from her to him for someone else or maybe she just wanted tot say good- bye to him.

It seems the spirits can perceive those who are receptive to them. But after seeing the girl from his school, Derrick told me he wanted the visions to stop; they frightened him too much.

"Once you stop them," I said, "you may never get them back. One day, you may want them."

He is seeing them for a reason that will be revealed in his future; of this I am sure. He has been set on his path for a purpose, just as I was set on mine.

I have wanted to write about these visions for quite a while now. But I didn't know if it would be possible to write about something which I truly do not yet understand. The path to this understanding and my reason for writing is to let others know that they are not alone.

There are more of us who see visions and spirits than you would think. We are unique, gifted, and far from being nut cases. We have insights into things people only wish they could experience, and that scientists wish they could explain. That visions may be caused by special brain waves when you sleep, is one possible explanation. But I must be asleep in the daytime, because they appear to me any time and everywhere! My only wish is, through this book, to guide those who are on a different spiritual path.

Chris is a very dear new friend in my life, I met her one day this past summer when she came into my store with her friends. We clicked right away, and when she told me about her trips to Salem, Massachusetts, we shared another common factor. I have always loved Salem and it was a special treat to meet an actual relative of one of the victims of the Salem Witch Trials. She visits Salem as often as she can on Halloween, and she stops in to see Rebecca Nurse's House. When Chris recently emailed me a picture, which I enlarged to put on my computer, I was surprised to discover what appear to be thirteen orbs, possibly spirits, in it!

As we talked more, I learned that there is a burial ground on the land near by, so they say, of the relatives that passed, including victim Rebecca Nurse, whose family removed her from the gallows the night of the hanging and returned to their land to lay her to rest. The Nurse family no longer owns the house, but because she is a family descendant, Chris will always be attached to it and to the land.

Sadly, this was not to be the last of the unfortunate events for relatives of the Nurse family. Chris's niece, Samantha was reported missing. Her disappearance made national news. To date, almost three years have passed and her location is still unknown.

I wanted so much then to help find this missing girl. Messages were coming through to me at night that I felt must have had something to do with Samantha, but I was unable to piece anything together. I was so frustrated to still be learning how to receive and interpret my messages. I was not able to help Chris to find her niece and was really upset and disappointed that Samantha couldn't be found in time to be home before the holidays and safe for the winter. I still occasionally receive messages concerning her.

After Father's passing, my brother and I were expecting him to appear in a vision to us, but instead, he visited another way. He came to me as a voice, his voice and with a message which I was told had to be communicated to my brother right then and there.

The first part of Dad's message came as an unusual sadness which rushed over me and provoked in me the feeling that I didn't want to be at my store any more. Although I wanted to leave immediately, I did not. I stayed alone in my store that evening, working on my web page, when my father came through with the next part of his message.

At the time it happened, I was not even thinking of him. I was concentrating of getting my web page just right. *I have a message for you,* said my Dad's voice clearly in my mind, startling me.

A chill pierced my body like stepping naked, into a blizzard, but it was the middle of July!

The message he gave had two parts connecting to the same subject: My nephews. He told me to tell my sister to encourage my nephew, Derrick's writing, and to tell my brother to stop drinking because he was destroying his children. I dutifully passed the messages along to my sister and my brother. They seemed to have fallen on deaf ears. But at Grandmother's funeral, my brother arrived unexpectedly sober. And he stayed sober the whole day.

When my store was operating, I just loved talking to the people who came in; some of them were even willing to share their own experiences. Once a lady came in who talked about being tapped on the shoulders. This happened often and terrified her and she wanted them to stop visiting her in that way.

In an effort to find a different way for them to communicate with her, we decided that at night time, when relaxed and nearly asleep, she should first ask them to come to her in a manner that is easier for her to understand, and not so startling. Her dreams had also been also been frightening and she had hoped by talking to me, to take home information for a better understanding.

People just need to know that they are not alone in their experiences. It's OK to be different. This type of "different" doesn't make you crazy; it just means you have spirit guides who want you to know they are there to support you. Although I do not consider myself a psychic, sometimes things come through in that way. I am not one who easily figures things out; the visions are not something I can switch on and off.

Spirits appear when and where they want to. I still can't figure out why.

Chapter Five

Helpers from Beyond

Uncle Walt passed away when I was about eighteen. I didn't know him well, but liked him, nevertheless. Once after his passing, he visited me with a message for his wife. I contacted her to relay the message as he had instructed. She was short with me and abruptly told me that she did not believe in any of this "stuff"; she only believed in Jesus.

"This doesn't require you to believe, just to listen," I told her. "Your husband's message is: I know what you did with my watch and it is OK."

She was silent; I waited for a moment.

"So what did you do with his watch?" I asked her.

She hesitated and then told me that on impulse, she had given it to his best friend, but had later wondered if it was the right thing to do. I thought to myself, *why, after years of isolation due to our difference in beliefs, did I waste my time contacting her?*

Why? Because Uncle Walt asked me to; and it was the right thing to do.

Uncle Walt is one of my guardians. He had a hand in helping me achieve my dreams! My best memories of Uncle Walt are of him and my aunt taking me to McDonalds and allowing me to order anything I wanted. One time I ordered six hamburgers!

My aunt watched as I unwrapped the first burger and shook her head in disbelief.

"She is not going to eat all six of them!" she said.

But food was scarce as we grew up, so the opportunity to get anything I wanted was a great thing indeed! (There had been times we were so hungry that we sat, not moving for hours, because we had no energy.) Of course, my eyes were bigger than my belly and I was only able to eat two of those six hamburgers. But because my uncle had insisted, I had gotten what I wanted! He seemed to know about the hunger, and on that day we connected and he became a favorite of mine.

My other grandmother (on Mom's) side also had a role in helping me with the store. The days of multi-tasking by managing the store, my web business, full time work and my book, were difficult. (There was no way I could have done this on my own, without some help from beyond.) Grandmother was not with me often, but I talked to her all the time, and thanked her for the many pennies she left me, which I constantly found in unusual places.

As a child, I remember her saying to me, "If everyone gave you a penny, you would be rich."

I felt she left me those pennies to help me toward that success. I still do talk to her whenever I can and often come across a shiny penny when I least expect it.

When we toured Salem, I fell in love with the town. It was so beautiful! It was difficult to believe this had been the site of so much violence so long ago. While there, we stayed at the Salem Inn. We spent the entire first day shopping and I went to bed exhausted that night. But I was rudely jolted awake by two dogs growling and pulling at my shopping bags, which I had set on the floor near our suitcases.

"Get, get!" I yelled at them. "Shoo!"

"Who are you yelling at?" my husband asked, now startled awake by my shouting.

"Those two dogs!" I replied, and went back to sleep.

That next day, we took the Salem tour, and during the tour guide's lecture on the history of Salem, we discovered that two dogs had also been accused of Witchcraft and subsequently, hung. My husband and I looked at each other a smiled. The dogs we had seen in our room the night before were most certainly these same dogs.

This vision had been an easy one to figure out. I reported this incident to the inn, because they are often asked if anything odd ever happens there. Well I can say that when conditions are just right, spirits can be seen there, as well as anywhere! I loved Salem.

My fascination with "witches" and "the craft" dates back to the age of sixteen. Although the word "witch" has evil connotations in today's world, being one and practicing the craft has been something I never doubted, like magic.

The first vision responsible for putting me on the path toward the craft occurred when I was in my early twenties. In that visitation, a wise, elderly lady appeared to me, dressed in black. She held out her hand and instructed me to burn a black candle, repeating it over and over. I didn't even know they made black candles!

Looking back, I remember that my life then was so very stressful! I was on my second marriage and second child. My ex-husband was trying to exert control over me by trying to keep my oldest daughter away from me. I was hammered with threats of court, and was asked for large sums of money or "I would not be able to see my daughter."

It reached the point where my new husband and I sadly had to resign to not being able to see her. The separation from her was unbearable and as a result of all this stress, my doctor placed me on anti-depressant pills. The whole situation affected my new family profoundly. My youngest daughter didn't understand why she couldn't be with her big sister. We all cried a lot, but eventually anger took over.

So after the visitation by the elderly lady dressed in black and out of desperation with nothing left to loose, I decided to "burn a black candle."

The hunt for a black candle was interesting and fun. I discovered its purpose was to help someone rid themselves of negative energy. I finally found one and burned it as the vision in black had instructed. The burning of that candle opened a whole new world for me.

The situation in my life abruptly changed for the better. To this day, I attribute that life-change to burning that black candle. Because of that positive result, I decided to do some research into candle magic and candle making. After a little trial and error, I soon learned how to make my own candles. I began mixing the contents with the intent to achieve specific purposes, and successfully sold them to a local new age store. This was long before I even thought of opening my own store. I so enjoyed selling my candles to this other store, that the thought of having a store of my own store had never even crossed my mind. When it eventually did occur to me, it seemed so far out of reach, that I immediately dismissed the idea.

But my life has always been spirit guided, with visions and messages. I have listened and they helped guide me to where I am now. One reason they keep appearing to me is to show me the way.

One particular spirit, who really kicked me into gear to fulfill my dream of opening my own store, was one who spoke to me in a strong manner.

I was home at lunchtime that day, and had taken our dog outside to do her business. As I came back into the house, I turned around to see a lady standing in the doorway, dressed in 1950's attire, with her hands on her little waist.

She held her arms out to her side and with a shrug said, "Are you ready?"

Her tone implied irritation and frustration. My initial thought was what the hell this lady is doing in my house! Then I felt the coldness in the air and the feeling I get when I get this visitors fell over me. I felt her being annoyed with me. Was it because of the delays in opening up my store? I froze! My dog sat down beside me and just stared at the spot where she was standing. Had he seen her also?

The Spirit soon vanished and then I said out loud, *Yes, I am ready!*

After a little family photo research, I discovered who this lady was. She was Mom's favorite aunt who had died in a car accident with her children. Her connection to me is through my Mom.

My brother, Chuck, and I had made a pact when we were small. Whenever either one of us would have a vision, we were to call each other. It's a big event between us; sometimes causing him to call me at midnight! It is still a mystery why others don't see things like we do. It happens so often now, that it has become a "normal" part of our lives.

For example, both my daughters saw me awaken on a recent Tuesday morning talking about my phone bill. How weird.

"There goes Mom again," they said to each other.

But a voice in my head had been saying, *Watch your phone bill, something is wrong.*

I remember thinking to myself, *Ok, I will,* then fell back to sleep. The voice woke me again, with the same message; I had to be told twice, for me to retain it as a real message. I just don't worry about my phone bill at 2 a.m.

Well, the next morning, I had remembered my message and out of curiosity, decided to go through the stack of mail I had picked up from the Post office the day before. How interesting! I had just received my cell phone bill, from a cell company I had used for approx 1 1/2 years. The average bill had ranged from $45.00 to $ 60.00. However, this one had a nice little bite to it at $199.00!

I contacted their customer service and brought this discrepancy to their attention. They attributed it to errors created by their new billing system, stating that other customers had gotten similar surprises in their phone bills. Although I probably would have noticed this billing error anyway, I think the spirits just wanted to again reassure me that they are present. That was confirmation enough for me.

Some people wonder, "If spirits really know what's going to happen, then why don't they give you the winning lottery numbers too?"

But they never do and never will.

And as a result of the phone bill incident, I figured out why.

I think it works this way: The phone bill had already happened and was a "done deal" by the time I received it, but a lottery drawing holds many variables and events that have not yet unfolded. Spirits don't really know the future; they just have access to some information about past events, which we don't.

Spirits warn me of stress, danger, of upcoming events and when someone is sending ill will my direction. The method which seems to be working the best for me is to first figure out the message and then figure out how to handle the situation created by the message. It's sort of like a detective game, I guess. I am truly happy to have such unique things happen in my life; I feel blessed.

Death, to me, is not a future event; the date is a done deal. Spirits know when a death is imminent. They visit us so we may see that they here to help and support us. A cheerful aspect of this side of spirituality is the opportunity to talk to people about it, sharing experiences and watching how they unfold.

Everyone has had unusual things happen to him or her. I remember one customer of mine who was frightened by her spirits and visions, but she still did not want to send them away. I think that sums it up for a lot of us who operate on an extrasensory level. I wouldn't change it for the world.

Chapter Six

A Collection of Visions

A few days before my grandmother passed away, my husband had a unique vision.

At home and well into the night, he awoke to hear a piano playing rather loudly. Thinking it was probably the TV; he got up and looked around the bedroom door and into our living room to investigate.

There by the fireplace, was a silver haired lady, playing an old upright piano. Trying to get her attention to get her to quiet down, he waved his arms at her. The lady glanced over at him and he noticed she wore glasses. Suddenly she disappeared before his eyes and the room began glowing with a foggy light, which went up the fireplace and reflected on the glass in the fireplace doors.

Shaken, but still sleepy, he went back to bed. The dogs then started to whimper and cry. He grumbled, but got up again to let them outside. But when he went to their beds to get them, he found them both still sound asleep! He gasped aloud and startled them. Well, the dogs were really awake now, so he took them outside and when they returned, put them back down for the night. My husband returned to the bedroom, a little more awake now and quite puzzled.

I think his exact words at the time were, "What the hell!"

The spirits don't usually appear to him, but this time they had to get a message to me and used him to do so. At the time, I was heavily preoccupied with events surrounding the disappearance of Samantha, my friend Chris's missing niece, mentioned earlier in this book.

Messages were coming to me all the time then, one especially, repeating over and over like a mantra, *where I fell, is where I lie.*

Although I remember the spirits trying to awaken me on many nights, I was exhausted from their constant interruptions and just wouldn't let them in. I was angry with them for bothering me so.

The next morning, Bill told me about the strange happenings with the piano lady and the dogs. In an effort to understand the message, I tried to analyze the incident in the same way one would analyze a dream. But the only person I ever knew who had a piano was, my grandfather from Dad's side, who had passed away many years ago. In my mind's eye, as he told me what he had seen, I heard the piano playing and found myself glancing down at my grandmother. It then seemed to me that the vision was really related to the passing of my grandmother.

"This is what your vision meant," I told my husband. "It all makes sense now," and began to explain my logic.

Father had a part in that vision, knowing that I would associate the piano with my grandfather. The lady with glasses, of course, would have to be my grandmother. The spirits were using Bill to get my attention. They were telling me by using the annoying loud piano, that they were going to continue to annoy everyone in the household until I let them in again. (The messages about Samantha stopped; but I never was able to solve the chanted riddle of "where I fell is where I lie.")

My aunt retold grandmother's last days to me. Because Grandmother couldn't care for herself anymore, my aunt, who was a very kind and special lady, took her in and took really good care of her for many years.

On this one particular day, near her end, Grandmother was calling, "Jack, Jack!"

My aunt ran into the room to see what was wrong, and told Grandmother that Jack had left. (Jack was my aunt's son, but also my grandfather's name.)

Grandmother angrily said, "Not *your,* Jack, My Jack! He just went into the bathroom. Go look!"

Puzzled, my aunt looked in the bathroom, to put Grandmother at ease.

"No, Mom. There's no one here," she said. Grandmother got really upset with her.

"Yes he is!" she argued.

My aunt said Grandmother had really believed Jack was there. My grandmother's experience, these few days before she passed, was very similar to what my father had seen while I was visiting him at the hospital in New Jersey shortly before he passed. They both saw visions of their loved ones who had passed on and returned now when a death was near. Maybe it's true that they come back to help you pass over.

I have not pinned down when spirits will appear or why. I certainly do not control them. They come when they want to or need to. They come in visions standing in front of me, or they wake me at night, either in plain sight, or as a voice in my head which says, *I have a message for you.* The message can either be for me or for someone else!

I learned quickly how to tell them, "Not tonight, you don't! I am tired!"

This technique works to avoid them for only a short while; they still succeed in getting their messages through at night, in my dreams. When that happens and I don't want to be disturbed by them, I am often able to interrupt my dreams and wake myself. But the next time I sleep and dream, the dreams become weirder and a little more off the beaten path, which makes understanding them even more difficult.

If you want to know the best way to analyze your dreams, you must first progress to the point where you can ask the spirits to communicate with you directly through your dreams. Understand first, that the true meaning of dreams can't be looked up in a book, unless the book is all about you!

Your dreams are in a code meant just for you and are not listed or explained in any basic dream interpretation book. You can purchase one only if you want to know just basic symbolic meanings, but in my experience, once I disregarded all those commercial dream books and looked inside myself to find what they really meant to me, I was able to analyze things more accurately.

If you want to learn to "look within yourself" for these meanings, you can simply start by writing down a list of one-word things that you remember from your dream, like: dog, black, tree, etc. List them in a column then return to this list a little later and write down what the word means to you. For example, a tree could mean growth to you, a dog could mean love, black could mean peaceful. Keep the meanings simple. Usually the correct interpretation is the first thought which pops into your mind after reading the word on your list.

I can confidently say that when you discover the meanings behind your dreams, you will improve many things in your life. Your thoughts will become centered, your relationships will stabilize and your life will become a calm place where you are glad to be. But you will have to figure these dream words out for yourself, first. It's not hard; just try and don't cave in to self-doubt.

In your life journey, you will discover people that will love to hear your visions and dreams; these same people make great sounding boards when you need a second opinion. I have found that talking about a dream helps crystallize its meaning.

For example, recently, for four nights in a row, I had a series of dreams that really stumped me.

One of the last dreams in this set of four "starred" me pointing to an airplane as it was flying over water and I was saying to a crowd, "Look, that plane is going down!"

Well, last night we learned that over Lake Erie, a small plane had just gone down with nine people aboard. I knew without a doubt, that I had seen this event in that dream. I wanted to run down to the Lake and see if I could help, but the crash was not in the same vicinity of Lake Erie as where I live. Besides, what could I have done? Although you are able to see an event like this, there is nothing you can do to prevent its occurrence.

Often I get messages that prepare me for change and when my dreams become very persistent, I know a major change is coming in my life. For example, for a week prior to hearing the news that the plaza where my storefront was located had been sold, I had nightly dreams. We vendors were aware the sale was a good possibility. We also knew the rent for our stores would increase when a new owner took over. But through these series of dreams, I had been told to prepare myself for change, and that the change was going to be costly; I need to save my money, now.

The first, in my series of four dreams, was of me flushing myself down the toilet. It seemed this was my normal way of transportation! I was going to the same place I always went, my store, but it was a little farther away than the current one. So I had to "flush" to get there on time.

Funny, I know. But when analyzed, the flush meant to me that I was removing the old water to replace it with the new. The "water" was my business, the old is going and new is coming; an old business is going and a new business is coming--a fresh start. I was not sad; I was happy to flush myself!

In a dream the very next night, I was sitting on my bed with my favorite cat Salem. He is my soul friend; he understands me without words. I was sitting on the bed and it was full of stacks and stacks of coins; I was leisurely rolling them up. Now when we usually do roll coins, it is for money to take with us on a big trip, or to an event. That dream was telling me to save my dimes, and that I had time!

The third dream, in my series of four, was about my husband and some risqué adult magazines, but then it switched to us buying a beautiful Victorian style house in Salem, right by the water. In the dream, we had to travel back to our current house to make sure everything for the sale was finalized. We had to talk to that new tenant renting my former house and heard how wonderful things were, and how cheap the rent was. Well, I didn't like her flirting with my husband and woke up.

The magazines and the flirting were my insecurities about this impending change. What if the store doesn't work with the new owner? What if I can't pay my higher rent? The bottom line in that whole dream was I was not alone, and that together with my family, my aspirations will come true. But I needed to step outside my comfort zone and "go for it." My house is my comfort zone, and my dreams reflect my fear at going further in debt for my business.

The last in my series of dreams was about an evil spirit. In this dream, I was equipped with a small shaker of sea salt and using the salt sparingly, I sprinkled it around some pool balls (the floating type for swimming pools), to encircle myself. Of course I ran out of the salt, and the evil spirit dragged me out of the circle and pulled me by the feet around to the next room, which was large and empty. I was not frightened or in any pain; I think I was actually laughing. I forced myself awake.

After some thought, I decided that this dream summed up the new events that would be taking place in my business; the new store owner and the possibility of closing of my store. I would be forced into a situation outside my comfort zone, and with this change, my world would change. I needed to venture beyond the protection of the circle of salt. If I had to be dragged and forced to make the move, then so be it.

All these dreams, taken as a whole, tell me clearly not to doubt my business skills or my other abilities, that indeed I do have a gift. Now what do I do with it?

If you are currently having dreams, please work with them. Don't pass them off as stupid. Even though they don't appear at first to make sense, piece them together. They will transform from a puzzle, into a picture. It will not be easy at first, but believe in your self and in your spirit guides. Ask them at night for answers and help. Mine have never disappointed me.

On a Monday in early November, I was settling in to start my live chat on my web site (which I no longer have) Our usual "chat meet" was scheduled for every Monday at 7 p.m. Eastern Time. There were some initial problems with getting signed in for the first chat, so I delayed the chat one week, sending everyone an email notifying them we would try again the following Monday night.

But there were a few of us die-hards who kept trying that night and some of us finally managed to get signed on. As it turned out, that was an especially good night to be in the chat meet, for on that night we had a special guest who also managed to log on.

We call her Glenda; she is known to our group and is a clairvoyant and psychic abilities. Because the chat group was so small that night, we each got to ask her a question. But when it was my turn, I told her that could feel the room around me turn cold and there was a strong hospital antiseptic smell was in the air. I knew something was going to happen.

That Monday night was the beginning of a long span sleeplessness, as I nightly had vivid dreams and received messages that made no sense to me at the time. By the end of the week, the visions were gaining more strength and were taking a more solid form.

It was Thursday night and I was almost asleep, when something caused me to open my eyes to find someone standing by my bed; I was startled and screamed. The vision vanished and after I finally calmed myself down, I slept fitfully until daylight.

The next night, Friday, I wasn't even fully asleep when the room started turning red. I moved closer to my husband, and thought to myself, *Oh no! Here we go again.* Because this has been happening to me since childhood, I knew that when the room turned red, it usually meant I was about to have a visitor. But no visitor came just then.

I was drifting off only to be awakened by the feeling of someone holding or restraining me. I had the distinct feeling of heat, like "burning up." A man's soft voice was talking to me and told me he was a fireman whose name was Jonathan. A word that sounded something like "Begone" kept coming into my mind; maybe it was his last name.

Angry at being disturbed again, I told him to be gone! I get irritable like that when I have back-to-back nights of "spirit" activity and little to no sleep. I was frightened because although I have seen and heard them, I had never actually felt them like that before. The physical feeling of heat that had been generated from this spirit was overwhelming and alarming.

For some reason, I related the fireman to the fall of the Twin Towers on 9/11. I felt that he had lost his life during that horrible event as he was trying to save someone. I never researched this too far, other than doing a quick internet search, but I did find there were a couple of firemen named Jonathan that had passed in the 9/11 tragedy.

The presence of this spirit, threw me off track, though. His message was meant for another event that had not yet revealed itself. Since he was connected to the Twin Towers, I extended the "tower" concept to the Tower card in the Tarot deck. This card indicates a loss in stability; complete and sudden change. I knew that my job situation probably would be changing, but wasn't sure how or when. Perhaps the release of this book could send me onto a different path.

After getting hardly any sleep at all that week, I finally had a chance to lie down Saturday afternoon for a nap. Only an hour had passed, when we received an unexpected and tragic phone call that our nephew who was only fourteen years old was being "emergency flown" to the hospital! A tree had fallen on his head while he was playing in the woods. His head injuries were extremely grave. We were stunned by the news.

We went to the hospital later that night and as I entered the waiting room and saw my nephew's mother, I flashed to a vision where everyone was in a room standing in front of a casket. At that instant, I knew he was not going to make it. I pushed the vision aside, hoping with all my heart that I was wrong.

The next day we went again to visit him. By this time he had endured three brain surgeries. He was still unconscious. I touched his leg; it was warm. He was fighting a low-grade fever at the time. Those who waited at the hospital, fought with each other throughout the night, seeking to assign blame for the accident. All prayed; some thought he would wake up and be fine, some just hoped for a merciful end. Everyone was worried, angry and confused.

On our drive home, my husband and I were silent. I stared aimlessly at the side of the road as we traveled. There, I saw a little boy dressed all in one color of light blue. Turning my head to see him better as we passed, I watched as he waved goodbye to me. I knew what this meant and my heart sank in my chest as I sank into my seat.

Along with the little boy's image came a voice that I had heard for many of nights now. The voice whispered that it was my job to let his mother know that he had no bandages or tubes where he was and that he was OK; he said to tell her good-bye.

Did I really see the boy? Were those thoughts really from him? After all this time of discovering and accepting my abilities, this was a time I needed to be absolutely correct before I spoke of what I had seen. I still just wasn't sure.

What if I was wrong and told his mother the message? She was already so distraught. I couldn't bear to put any more of a burden on her; especially if there was any chance I was wrong. I didn't tell her right away; I thought I was putting words in my own head for some reason. Maybe I finally had lost my mind.

The nights of sleeplessness didn't stop and neither did the message for his mother. As we maintained a daily vigil at the hospital, it came to the point that whenever I would talk to my nephew's mother, his spirit would yell for me to tell her <u>now</u>! I finally agreed; I would tell her as soon as the time was right.

I told her I needed to talk to her and as soon as we got a chance; she immediately knew I had a message for her. We walked out into the hall from the waiting room and I told her, as I had promised him I would. She sighed as if the weight of the world was lifted off her shoulders. She thanked me with tears in her eyes and we both returned to the crowd in the waiting room.

I am still amazed at how this little boy's spirit was so quickly able to find me to communicate for him; his body lingered for over a week in the hospital before finally giving up. But his spirit had already left his body when I saw him alongside the road. Although he was still tied to the physical world by his body, he hung around, still giving gifts of comfort and hope to those who were spiritually open enough for him to touch them.

This tragic experience, from which nothing good could have possibly come, presented me with a self-discovery for which I had been searching many years. My loving nephew, this little boy dressed in hospital blue waving to me from the roadside, presented me with the gift of realization. There is no doubt now, that the purpose of my gift is to receive messages from the dead and relay them to the living, as they ask me to do.

My nephew passed away on November 16th and was buried November 20th. He was only fourteen. We will miss him always.

Things started up again on December 5th. I was drifting to sleep that night, feeling so comfortable and suddenly sat bolt upright to find a lady standing beside my bed. She was a motherly figure very peaceful and calm. Of course I did what anyone else would if they found someone standing by their bed at night, I screamed.

I didn't understand what she wanted, and over the next few days I put the vision to the back of my mind, just letting it go, in a way. Two nights passed without incident but then I awoke to find a little girl was standing by my bed.

"Why do I have to see these people at night?" I angrily blurted it out. I didn't really mean to hurt their feelings but I would so like to have a good night's sleep!

I went to work the next day and told my friend about the two visitors. I didn't yet connect them to her until the following night.

Upon falling asleep that night, I heard in my head, *the messages are for Maura.*

They just wanted me to pass their message on to my friend from work. These two spirits, a mother and daughter, were killed in a tragic car accident the previous week over the Thanksgiving holidays and were connected to my friend. The mother spirit was an ex-sister in law and the daughter spirit was an ex-niece.

My friend told me that according to the family, her ex-niece had just become engaged and the wedding had been set for early next year. I heard mournful crying in my head; the daughter was not ready to accept that she had passed on. Her mother though, accepted death and passed on peacefully.

I had two jobs with this message. One was to help the daughter find her closure so she could move on. The other was to reunite the daughter with her mother.

I told my friend, who was the mother's ex-sister-in-law, about this new message and described the surroundings the daughter had shown me. There was a smell of something sweet burning, reminding me of burning pancakes, and a feeling of a comfortable home atmosphere, like at a grandmother's house. My friend recognized immediately where this place was. The daughter was still at her home; the grandmother was there to help with the funeral proceedings and was making breakfast for the other family members present. My friend said the grandmother was famous for burning pancakes.

It disturbed me though, that the daughter was not moving on. Days later, I could still hear her crying. At the time, I was not really sure what to do, and I suggested to my friend, that we let her hang out till after the holidays. If her mom had not yet convinced her to let go of this world, I would have to try. I hoped her mom would succeed.

Her crying in my head was a low, muffled sound and it was heart-breaking. I was driving to work the other day and for no reason, I just started crying. I had no clue then as to why, but I know now that I was an outlet for her unrelenting sorrow.

Chapter 7

It Runs in the Family

My youngest brother, Chuck, has enough of his own stories to write another book. I know he doesn't always like the events, but it definitely runs in the family! I don't know how many times he has called me in the middle of the night to describe some incident that has just happened.

My brother hunts, and had many guns as he was growing up for deer hunting and other small game. One time, as he was sighting in a particular gun, he had the scope up by his eye, loaded, when something told him to put the gun down. As he started lowering the gun, the trigger caught and fired; blowing the gun to pieces.

They found a thick, large piece of the gun in the middle of the roadway, many yards away from the target practice firing range. Had he not moved that gun away from his head, he would no longer have been with us. He and I both believe that his spirit guide was looking out for him just then; it wasn't "his time" yet.

Sometimes a thing will pop into your thoughts and you ignore it, making a decision about a certain issue; a decision which was not based on the particular feeling provoked by that thought. Often, you later discover that had you paid attention to that feeling, you would have made a better decision. Learning what to act upon and what to ignore seems to be the hardest part.

Those little feelings and thoughts that come into your head are spirit driven. They are not evil thoughts, they are guidance. Spirit guided thoughts would never tell you to harm anyone. They only instruct; they just tell you to turn left, when you were going to turn right. They are not connected to any evil, or anyone's acts of violence that would cause harm to another or yourself. This is just like the inner voice of support, like your conscience. We have all experienced it. If you need guidance in a situation, ask your spirit guides to help you out, and maybe things will just go the way you hope!

Chuck tells stories going back to when he was in fifth or sixth grade and he can still remember them like they happened yesterday.

After my father got out of the Military, we moved from N.A.S Lemoore, to Bridgeton, New Jersey. The house that we rented there already had its own haunting stories. I don't know if any of them were true; we never really investigated them. But some events throughout our childhood caused us to think the stories might have had some merit.

My brother remembers sleeping on the couch one night and awaking suddenly to find himself floating up off of the couch. I thought it was probably just an astral travel event, where people leave their bodies to travel, but my brother insisted that he was awake and in his body. There was only air beneath him as he looked down onto the couch below. He panicked when he realized what was happening and dropped heavily back onto the couch. He had no explanation for that event.

He has had other experiences with noises waking him up. One particular noise he remembered was of someone walking up the steps from the basement. Their footfalls sounded like they were wearing "Romper Room" cups on their feet. For those of you that may not remember what "Romper Room" cups were, they were like a plastic cup with strings which you would stand on and walk around with, using the strings to hold the cups against your feet. The footsteps came up the basement steps, into the kitchen and then back down the steps. He had no explanation for this event either.

When Chuck would call me at midnight or in the wee hours of the morning, I always knew something odd was going on.

One summer, my family and I stayed at Chuck's house during a visit to the New Jersey area. After we returned home, my brother called and reported that he had started seeing and feeling weird things at his house.

Chuck was working down in the basement of his new house, while the rest of the family slept. He often did this, as he had problems sleeping due to chronic pain from back injuries. This night, working alone downstairs, he was startled to see his cat, Smokey Bear, race down the stairs, and curl up on a rug near Chuck. This was decidedly odd behavior for the cat; he seemed to have been frightened by something and had run downstairs to find someone to protect him.

Chuck looked up from the cat and was about to begin working again, when he was interrupted by a blast of really cold air from behind, which seemed to pass entirely through him. He instantly knew he and the cat were not alone in the basement.

A little shaken, he continued with his work. A short time passed and he heard a big bang upstairs, and went upstairs to see what on earth his wife was doing. When he got upstairs, he found his wife was still asleep.

Still trying to locate the source of the noise, he went into the living room and found what had been a very securely mounted and large picture of his wife's father, now lying on the floor. For that huge picture to have just fallen off its hook was impossible, as the picture need to be lifted up and out of the mounting, to be removed from the wall.

He woke his wife so she could see what happened to the picture and phoned me shortly afterward. During our conversation that night, I found out that Chuck's wife's father had a birthday coming up. He had passed away the year before and she had been thinking about him, missing him. He just stopped by for a visit to let Diane know he was there and that he had heard her. The house returned to normal after that night.

On another night, Chuck was down in his basement folding laundry, when he again felt the room suddenly turn cold, sweeping through him like stepping into a meat freezer. Shivering, he became aware of a man's voice coming from the basement's far corner, calling his name.

"Chuck. Chuck."

Well needless to say, my brother bolted up the stairs as fast as he could move, which is just not fast enough when you have back injuries and you need to get moving quickly! We have a good laugh about these things now.

But Chuck's visitors are not only in the basement. It's not just the place that draws them to you, it's you. I believe they are attracted to you because they know that you are open to them.

On a recent evening, he recalled going into his bathroom, which is located in his master bedroom. As the room was lit by the streetlight outside, for privacy, he closed the bathroom door and then turned on the bathroom light. He brushed his teeth, turned off the light and opened the bathroom door to go to bed, but stopped in his tracks. He saw a figure, which at first glance he thought was his wife.

"Sorry," he said. "I didn't know you had to get in there."

But as he looked more closely at the figure, the focus "cleaned up" around it and he became aware that this was a male figure. Thinking this was an intruder, he took a swing at him and watched, horrified, as his fist went right through. We never did figure out what that spirit's message was, or even who it was.

Do they always have a message? I guess every event is different. I am going to believe that they have found me for a reason. I hope in time, to gain a deeper understanding of them.

I am happy with any way the spirits choose to come to me. Some times months will pass without an event. Once I went almost a year with no visits. But just as soon as I think they are all finished coming to me, a visitor will appear, just to let me know they are still around. So if you see the spirits and worry because they haven't visited you in a while, rest assured that once they know you're receptive to their messages, they will continue communicating with you. You only see what you re able to handle.

To date, I have not yet learned to turn this ability on or off at will. I have only been able to tell the spirits to come another night or have asked them to come to me in dream form instead of actually appearing before me during the night.

I had interesting, but suspicious offers from people who said they could stop the spirits from coming through to me, but I refused such offers. This ability is part of me and this is who I am. This is what makes me different from so many and creates a common ground with so many others.

I hope that my story will be heard for it is my story of awakening. I wish to awaken those who have similar gifts and earnestly hope that this book will help at least one person attune to the worlds surrounding them.

For those of you just beginning the path of awakening and for those of you already on it, please help as many living souls as you can through those communications from the deceased souls beyond.

They, who have gone before, are still here.

And always will be.

Made in the USA
Middletown, DE
16 April 2022

63955758R00043